52
PROGRAMS
THAT POP

A YEAR OF FUN PROGRAMMING FOR SENIOR ADULTS IN NURSING HOMES, ADULT DAYCARE, AND CHURCH GROUPS

By
Debbie Ann Scott

"52 Programs That Pop:A year of fun programming for senior adults in nursing homes, adult daycare, and church groups," by Debbie Ann Scott. ISBN 978-1-62137-694-1(Softcover) 978-1-62137-695-8 (eBook).

Cover Design by Bearded Bee Designs.

Published 2015 by Virtualbookworm.com Publishing Inc., P.O. Box 9949, College Station, TX 77842, US. ©2015, Debbie Ann Scott. All rights reserved. No part of this publication may be reproduced, stored in a retrieval system, or transmitted in any form or by any means, electronic, mechanical, recording or otherwise, without the prior written permission of Debbie Ann Scott.

FOREWORD

I would like to thank my wonderful husband for encouraging me to write this book and for his editorial suggestions. The colorful and fun cover was designed by my talented graphic designer son (see www.BeardedBeeDesigns.com). I want to thank my daughter who is always supportive of anything new that I want to try. God has blessed me with a wonderful, supportive family who are a constant source of joy.

INTRODUCTION

All of my professional career I have enjoyed creating compelling programs for senior adults. As an Activities Coordinator fresh out of a masters' program in Gerontology, I found myself with the responsibility of planning and implementing activities for 80 residents of the Asbury Methodist Village Nursing Home in Gaithersburg, MD. It was challenging to think of fun, interesting activities each month and provide programs that the residents would enjoy attending and participating in each week. I must admit, that there were times when the creative juices weren't flowing quickly enough. There were other times when the press of meetings and the abundance of documentation required for group and one-on-one visits or when planning time was limited due to group programs, the one-on-one programming for the bed-bound residents left time for planning consistently awesome programs challenging. In time, I found myself planning programs at home on my own. There just were not many printed resources to call upon to help with the planning. Someone should write a book, I thought.

In time, our family would relocate to a different state. Before too long, I would serve as the Director of Senior Adult and Children's Ministries at Colonial Avenue Baptist Church in Roanoke, VA. Directing activities for both seniors and children gave me over a decade to perfect programming and activities techniques. I discovered what worked and what didn't.

Great programs for seniors work on several levels. They include learning, inspiration, and fun. Great programs and activities challenge seniors to give it a try, and even learn a new talent. Great programs often call upon several of the senses including touch, vision, hearing, taste and smell. Great programs can be entertaining but they also can be service-oriented. Art projects, craft projects, brain teasers, singing, storytelling, and reminiscing all play a helpful role. One of my favorite projects involved knitting hats for premature babies in the local hospital. Another involved making doll clothes and dressing dolls for a local charity to give to needy children at Christmas. Great programs and activities for seniors can entertain, educate, inspire, and connect seniors to the community, to their family, and to each other.

Senior adult directors have a challenging task. Some days a group leader's time and ideas are scarce. I put this book together to help those who lead senior adults have a resource with workable ideas that you and your seniors will look forward to and enjoy. I hope you will have as much fun with this book as I have had creating 52 programs that pop!

JANUARY

Theme: Hat Day

Decorate with a variety of hats. You can order some from Oriental Trading or pick them up at a craft store. Have the participants wear different hats to the program.

Food:

- Cake or cupcakes sitting on poster board circles to look like top hats for a celebration. Coffee & Tea

Craft:

- Get visors or ball caps to have participants decorate.

History:

Hats have always been an accessory that draws attention, accents and makes the wearer stand out. In the past, hats were worn by the elite to draw attention and set them apart as a person of wealth and influence. The first hat appeared in 3200 BC in Thebes tomb pictures. These pictures had a men wearing coolie straw hats. In 70 BC, a fur and feather headdress, called a chieftain, belonging to a young Danish lad appeared. We know this style hat as a headdress worn by Native Americans.

Next to come on the scene were felt hats in 50 – 818AD. The legend states that St. Clement used felt in his shoes to soothe and protect his feet as he walked. He noticed that it kept his feet warm and dry so he decided to make hats out of the felt to keep his head warm. This new hat design was successful and he also noticed that his hat would keep his body heat in too. Hatters in Ireland began making felt hats for this purpose and they became quite popular.

The title, *milliners,* was coined in 1529AD when they started making hats in Milan and Northern Italy.

Haberdashers companies were popping up that made and imported all types of hats to accent men and ladies outfits. Many new styles were being invented which included the top hat. In fact in 1797AD the top hat started a riot when John Hetherington wore it in public. Hetherington was even fined $500 for the riot his hat caused. This famous style of hat was even worn by our 16th President, Abraham Lincoln and it became his trademark look.

In 1865 AD the hat known as, the Stetson was developed and named after the creator John B. Stetson. This cowboy style hat is worn by many not just in Texas or out West, but all across the globe. Cowboy style hats are worn by farmers, businessmen and singers as an accent to their outfits or to give their look character.

The next arena were a large number of different hats are worn is the Kentucky Derby. In 1875AD you would see ladies adorning hats of all styles with feathers, bows, and flowers. Men wore straw and trilby hats, or capps. This tradition continues today. Many women plan their Derby hat for months before the event.

In America hats show up everywhere. We even see them on Presidential Inauguration Days. In fact Aretha Franklin was featured in TIME magazine when she wore a stunning hat to an Inauguration Day. Even Jacqueline Kennedy, wore her famous "pill box" style hat at her husband's Inauguration and started a trend among the ladies as they began wearing the pill box style hat. Another famous lady, Princes Diana, was famous for her lovely hats at all Royal occasions, and her classy look was enjoyed by all.

Church services can also give occasion to hat-wearing. Easter Sunday seems to be a favorite day to sport a lovely bonnet or hat that compliments an outfit.

Hats are a fun accessory that everyone can wear to dress up an outfit, draw attention to themselves or just to accent your character with a style of your own.

Activities:

- Have hats or pictures of hats on display and have the participants determine the kinds of people who uses that type of hat. Examples might include a chef's hat, jockey hat, hard hat, motor cycle helmet, top hat, beret, fire hat, cop hat, service hat, derby, ball cap, etc. How many hats can you find?

- Invite participants to wear a hat to the program and tell about the hat they are wearing.

- Perhaps participants can draw a picture of their favorite hat and tell a story about it. Did anything funny happen when you wore a hat?

Theme: Elvis' Birthday Anniversary

Have Elvis music playing and maybe photos of Elvis over the years.

Food:
- Make the room into a 50's Soda Shop and serve Coke Floats
- Peanut Butter and Banana Sandwiches

Craft:
- Make a guitar. Get empty tissue boxes and stretch rubber band around the box long wise. Put a piece of dowel rod or folded cardboard for the saddle or bridge (the part where the strings rest) under the rubber bands on one side of the top. Pluck your homemade guitar.
- Search *Pinterest* for the guitar card

History:
The first Rock and Roll star who turned the music world on its head was Elvis Presley. Growing up in Tupelo, Mississippi he was exposed to many types of music, and his music showed a mix of blues, gospel, and country. What brought him so much attention in the 50's was the sensual swivel hip movement that went along with his compelling singing. This hip action drew the teenagers and began a generation of rebels and misbehaving teens. Most adults felt he was vulgar and a bad influence for their children, but his sweet melodic voice won the battle and it changed the culture of music and singers performances.

Let's learn a little about Elvis, who he was and how he grew up. Born January 8, 1935, in East Tupelo,

Mississippi, Elvis was the son of Gladys and Vernon Presley. His father was a truck driver and his mom sewed for a living. Elvis was a twin, but Jesse Garon Presley was stillborn so Elvis grew up as an only child. When Elvis was three his father and two other employees changed this boss's check from $3 to $8 and cashed it at a local bank. Vernon plead guilty and they sent him to Parchment Farms Penitentiary where he served three years. While in prison Vernon's boss called in the Presley families house note, forcing Elvis and Gladys out of the family home. Gladys was forced to move in with Vernon's parents while Vernon was in prison for eight more months. After prison, Vernon's had a hard time holding down a job, consequently his family didn't have much to live off of.

The Presley family attended the First Assembly of God Church where his love of music began. The family even sang as part of their service to the Lord. Elvis' singing didn't stop at the church. His fifth grade teacher, Oleta Grimes encouraged Elvis to enter the talent contest at the Mississippi-Alabama Fair and Dairy Show on children's day. As he stood on a chair to reach the microphone, dressed in a cowboy suit, Elvis won second prize, and $5, for his rendition of Red Foley's "Old Shep." Along with the money he had free tickets to all the rides at the fair. After that day his love for music continued and on his birthday the following January, he received a guitar purchased from the Tupelo Hardware Store, and his Pastor Frank Smith, and his uncle Johnny Smith gave him basic guitar lessons.

In 1948 his dad lost another job, so Vernon moved his family to Memphis where Gladys brother got him a job at the Precision Tool Company. The Presley's moved to 370 Washington Street, a small apartment costing $11 a week.

September of that year Elvis enrolled at L.C Humes High School. He was a sophomore that year and he enjoyed working in the school library and Loew's State Theatre after school. In 1951 he got his driver's license, joined the Humes High School ROTC's and tried out for the football team which he didn't make because he wouldn't cut his sideburns and duck-tail hairdo. He enjoy venturing to Beale Street, the black section of town, where he learned gospel and spiritual style songs. In 1953 Elvis graduates from Humes High, at the age of 18, majoring in Shop, History, and English. His dad was proud and gave him his first car, a 1942 Lincoln Zephyr.

After graduation he secured a job at Parker Machinists Shop, but by June he was working at Precision Tool Company where he drove a truck for Crown Electric Co. He moved up quickly from stock boy to truck driver. During that time is when he changed his hair do to the pompadoured style. He never gave up on his music and that summer he recorded "My Happiness" and "That's When Your Heartaches Begins" at the Memphis Recording Studio where want-a-Be's could record their songs for $4.

Elvis continued recording in January 1954 with his song "Casual Love Affair" and "I'll Never Stand In Your Way," and "Without You" with Sam Phillips recording studio. Despite his attempts at fame he failed miserably. Phillips employed him to sing in his studio, wanting a white man who could sing negro spiritual songs. Later Phillips formed a band with Elvis, Scotty Moore as guitarist, and Bill Black as bassist. Unbeknownst to Phillips these three had been practicing together for a long time and on July 5, 1954, they recorded "I Love You Because," "Blue Moon of Kentucky," and "That's All

Right." Two days later Dewey Phillips, a Memphis DJ played "That's All Right" on his radio show WHBQ and audiences loved it. That night Dewey Phillips had Elvis on a live interview at the station and his career took off. That night Scotty Moore became his manager and "That's All Right" and "Blue Moon of Kentucky" became his first two hit songs. On September 25 that year Elvis made his first and last appearance at the Grand Ole Opry.

In 1955, Elvis appeared on the popular radio show Louisiana Hayride, and his television debut with the Hayride broadcast. Two other songs were rising to the top, "Good Rockin' Tonight" and "I Don't Care if the Sun Don't Shine." Memphis was buzzing with Elvis hits. Elvis successful career continued and in 1956 RCA records recorded "Heartbreak Hotel" in Nashville, Tennessee and he became a national star. He continued to record hit songs and appeared on Milton Berle, Steve Allen and Ed Sullivan television shows which boosted his career even further.

On March 24, 1958, Elvis joined the Army, but still continued to have hit songs. Five months later he took leave to be with his mother who was very ill. She died the day after he returned home. He felt this was the biggest tragedy in his life.

Soon to follow was when Priscilla swept Elvis off his feet and in May of 1967 they were married in Las Vegas. They had one child Lisa Marie. Elvis' career was bigger than life making millions of dollars touring and doing shows. Although he was in Vegas, he didn't gamble, he said it was against his Southern Baptist beliefs and up-bringing. He continued to draw larger and larger crowds which led him down a path of destruction for his marriage and his career. At the age of 42, Elvis was found by his girlfriend Ginger Alden dead in his bathroom at Graceland. A sad end to a wonderfully talented man's career. His songs are still enjoyed by many to this day and still has many fans who follow Elvis impersonator shows to relive the music and shows of the King of Rock and Roll – Elvis Presley.

Activities:

- Sing Karaoke of Elvis songs.
- Have an Elvis impersonator contest with the participants or bring in a professional Elvis impersonator.

Theme: Betsy Ross

Betsy Ross' birthday anniversary – January 1

Decorate with the original 13 colony US flags, and flags throughout the years. Surf the web for photos of the flags and Betsy Ross.

Food:

- Make a sheet cake and frost it with cool whip or vanilla icing. Then arrange blueberries in the upper left corner with mini marshmallows for stars. Slice strawberries or raspberries in half and use for the red strips of the flag.

- Another option is to take skewers and load with sliced strawberries, banana slice, rotating all the way up. On a few of the skewers put blueberries on the top. Arrange on a tray so that it makes an American Flag. (Hint: make sure you cut the bananas the same width. You can also use marshmallows for the white strip)

Craft:

- Make original flags from red, white and blue, felt, cloth, or construction paper. Purchase star stickers or make a star pattern for tracing.

History:

When you hear the name Betsy Ross, you immediately think of the maker of the American Flag. Born January 1, 1752 as Elizabeth Griscom. But she was married three times changing her name to Elizabeth Ashburn, Elizabeth Claypoole and finally Elizabeth Ross. Elizabeth's name was later shortened to Betsy which is what everyone recognizes her today as - Betsy Ross.

Let's look at how Betsy got to her flag-making career. Betsy was born to Samuel and Rebecca Griscom in Philadelphia, Pennsylvania, number eighth of seventeen children. Being part of a large family, plain wardrobes and strict rules were part of her upbringing. Her great-aunt Sarah Elizabeth Ann Griscom taught her how to sew. Her great-grandfather Andrew Griscom emigrated from England in 1680 and was a Quaker carpenter. Which also added to her strict upbringing.

Betsy attended Quaker public school, and upon graduation she was given an apprenticeship with William Webster a local upholsterer. This job not only taught her a trade, it was where she met John Ross, whom she would later marry. John was an assistant rector at Christ Episcopal church. John and Betsy eloped in 1772 causing turmoil in her family. Since John was not Quaker, Betsy was expelled from the Quaker church separating her from her family. The young married couple joined the Christ church which was where George Washington, the first President, worshiped and where they became friends. John and Betsy started their own upholstery business which was very successful. Although they were happily married they never had any children.

After only two years of marriage, the American Revolutionary War broke out. Ross was a member of the local militia and was killed at his post. Betsy, only 24 years old, continued in the upholstery business repairing uniforms, making tents and blankets. She also worked for the Continental Army by stuffing paper tube cartridges with musket balls.

Betsy was a young beautiful widow and she caught the eye of Carl von Donop. This was a distraction for him in the Battle of Iron Works Hill, and it kept him out of the Battle of Trenton.

Her second marriage was to Joseph Ashburn on June 15, 1777. Ashburn's was shipped out and he was captured by the British frigate and charged for treason and imprisoned in England at Old Mill Prison. While in prison he discovered his wife was pregnant with their daughter Eliza. Unfortunately he was never released and died in prison and never saw his daughter.

Six years later she met and married John Claypoole who met Ashburn in prison and was the person who told her about his death. They married in May 1783 and had five daughters. Claypoole moved his family to a larger house on 2nd street. He became ill and suffered for two decades before he passed in 1817. Betsy continued work in the upholstery business for 10 more years. When she retired she lived with Suzanna, her daughter in Abington, PA outside of Philadelphia.

Ross was having problems with her sight, and spent her last three years of life blind. At that time she had moved in with her daughter, Jane. She died at the age of 84 in Philadelphia, Pennsylvania, January 30, 1836.

So now that we know a little about Betsy Ross' life, how did she come about to make the first American Flag? The National Museum of American History researched where the first United States flag came from and recovered this story. The mention of Ross making the first flag was in 1870 when William Canby, her grandson, presented a paper to the Historical Society of Pennsylvania claiming she made the first flag for the United States. Canby claimed that he received his information from his aunt Clarissa Sydney (Claypoole) Wilson in 1857. Canby's dates corresponded with the historic journey George Washington took to Philadelphia in1776. A year later Congress passed the Flag Act. This historical account was the proof that Betsy Ross was chosen by George Washington to hand make the first flag of the United States. Betsy Ross was considered a major woman contributor to patriotism for our American History.

Activities:

- Surf the internet for trivia of what the different parts and colors of the flag stand for.
- Search how to display the American flag.
- Look for how to care for the flag, fold, and how to dispose of a damaged or torn flag.

First Flag

The next flag

Theme: Popcorn Day

Food:

- Popcorn, caramel popcorn, cheese popcorn, and popcorn balls. Variety of sodas.

Crafts:

- Popcorn Topiary - Get Styrofoam ball, skewer sticks, oasis, moss and small clay pot for each participant. Pop popcorn enough for each participant to cover the ball with popcorn using Tacky glue to glue it on. After the ball is covered with popcorn let it rest to dry. While the ball is drying, paint the skewer green. Put the oasis in the flower pot so that it will hold the skewer and popcorn ball up. You can decorate the flower pot with buttons, ribbon or paint if you wish. When popcorn ball is dry put the skewer into the ball and then put the other end into the flower pot. Add moss to cover the oasis. Then you will have a popcorn topiary.

- Popcorn balls – you will need the following for each participant: Popcorn (1/2 cup kernels or one 3.5-ounce package plain microwave popcorn) Marshmallows (1 10-oz bag), & Butter (1/4 cup). You can also add candy corn, M&M's, nuts or raisins. Grease your hand with butter and begin forming your popcorn ball in a plastic bowl using your hands. It won't take long to set up and then you can eat them or save for later in wax paper. Directions: Pop your corn, melt butter in a bowl in the microwave for 50 sec, next melt you marshmallows for one minute at at time until smooth. Next fold your popcorn into the mixture, adding other items if you would like. Next, form your ball and let cool. Enjoy!

History:

There are legends from the farmers out West that said that one summer it got so hot that the corn on the stalk popped right off the ear of corn in the field. Many of the animals thought it was snowing and lay down and died.

An Indian legend states that there are spirits within every kernel of corn and when they took the cobs inside their homes the heat would anger the spirits. The hotter the house got the more angry the spirits became until they finally popped, which released the spirits in a puff of steam within the house.

Both of these legends are fun but not true by any means. But you would find farmers and Indians growing corn which earned the corn the name of "prairie gold." Corn was a staple in their diets at that time as well as feed for the animals.

The oldest recorded findings of popcorn was found in the Bat Cave occupied by cave people near New Mexico three thousand years ago. Two Harvard graduates, Herbert Dick an anthropologist and Earle Smith a botanist discovered these findings while researching this area. As they dug down within the dirt they found tiny cobs of popcorn and upon further research they were even able to pop the kernels making popcorn.

In the 4th century pictures from the Zapotec tribes found drawings depicting popped corn within their headdresses and pictures of Maize gods holding popped corn in vessels. These drawings were pre-Inca civilizations located on the north coast of Peru.

Pueblo Indians, who settled in southwest Utah, had popped corn in the caves where they lived too. The earlier tribe was not the only ones who had popped corn in their diet, these inhabitants had it in the 10th century as well.

Spanish explorer, Hernando Cortes invaded Mexico in the 16th century and found popcorn as the food source of the Aztec Indians. He also found popped corn as decorative ornamentation within their headdresses and other items to adorn their outfits as they had celebratory dances and ceremonies.

Popped corn did not end in the 16th century. French explorers in the 17th century found Iroquois Indians who settled in Great Lakes region of the United States used corn for soups, entrees and desserts. In October of 1621, the English settlers joined with the Indians to hold the first Thanksgiving. Among the dishes that were prepared for this feast was popped corn, parched corn and rice corn. Popped corn was also used as a breakfast staple as a cereal topped with sugar and cream.

The 18th century came the development of the popped corn machine. Charles Cretors, from Chicago, Illinois developed this machine in order to sell popcorn on the street. Workers and sight-seers could enjoy this wonderful smell of the cooking corn and could purchase it on the spot for a snack. The early popcorn machines used gasoline burners for their heat source, but today we just need to use electricity to create this wonderful treat. Families would use a big soup pot with oil and kernels in the bottom and shake it over a kitchen stove heating the kernels until they popped. When they heard the popping sound stop, they knew it was ready to enjoy. Some eat the popped corn with salt and butter but some eat it plain.

During WWII American's sent sugar overseas for the troops. They mixed this with popcorn and made a popular treat replacing the limited production of candy at that time. After the war, popcorn consumption increased as movies and television viewing grew in popularity. A box or a bowl of popcorn is an easy treat to enjoy and share with the family.

Activities: Prepare ahead of time to allow color to dry on popcorn kernels

- Color popcorn kernels. Take popcorn kernels and mix food coloring in the bowl with one bag of kernels per color. Let dry thoroughly. Copy outlines of butterflies and glue them onto poster board. Cover the work area with newspaper before starting to keep the colored kernels from coming off onto the table. Use the different colors of kernels to glue onto the butterfly outline in a design of your choice.

- Have a pop-up story session. Let participants pop-up and tell a one or two minute story about the best popcorn they ever ate.

Theme: National Hug Day

Food:

- Twisted Pretzels that look like hugging arms. Pretzels can be dipped in chocolate and decorated or dipped in cheese or mustard.

Crafts:

- Fill a small mason jar with Hershey Hugs. Decorate the jar with ribbon, puff paint or other items and top with a sign that say; "Hugs for Hope," "Hugs for Health," "Hugs for Happiness" or other catchy saying.

History:

National Hug Day is an annual holiday founded on January 21, 1986, by Rev. Kevin Zaborney who was from Caro, Michigan. Hug Day was accepted by many countries and has spread to Canada, England, Australia, Germany and Poland. The main idea of National Hug Day is to encourage people to show affection with a hug for their family and friends. When you hug someone there is a mental and physical health benefits.

Health benefits from hugging are many. Hugs have been proven to help build a good immune system, decrease the risk of heart disease, and decrease levels of the stress hormone, especially in women. Hugs help reduce the harmful effects of stress while reducing blood pressure and heart rate. Hugs have been shown to improve overall mood and increase nerve activity. Hugs have positive immediate anti-stress effect, slowing breathing and heart rate which helps to calm you. Hugs boost oxytocin levels, which reduces the feelings of loneliness and anger. They also stimulates the thymus gland, which aids in the production of white blood cells and releases the dopamine in your body, which is known as the pleasure hormone. A hug can help you sleep and reduce pain.

Research has shown that babies and children without physical contact fail to thrive. Linda Blair, a clinical psychologist at Bath University, found hugging has a positive effect on children's emotional development. Hugs create a bond that allows a child to feel secure and connected to their parents. This feeling of trust helps with their ability to communicate. Hugs build self-esteem. Children in loving families are imprinted with a sense to love themselves and are able to connect with others.

Hugs are like meditation and laughter. Susmita Baral in his Lifestyle article, "National Hug Day 2014: 4 Scientific Reasons Why Hugging Is Good For You," determined that we all need hugs. He learned in his study that we all need 4 hugs a day for survival, 8 for maintenance, and 12 for growth. But when he asked his daughter how many hugs do you need a day? She replied, "I'm not going to tell you how many I like, but it's way more than eight." From her response he realized how important hugs are to life. (**Lifestyle** National Hug Day 2014: 4 Scientific Reasons Why Hugging Is Good For You By Susmita Baral, Jan 21 2014, 01:43PM EST)

Another researcher and relationship coach, Mihalko Baczynski, states that a hug effects your body and soul, making individuals feel special and loved. Hugs have no negative side effects, are free and natural. Researchers at the University of North Carolina shows that hugs increase the hormone and Oxytocin reduces blood pressure. Their researcher found that Oxytocin creates a caring bond between the people hugging. And that hugs are an inexpensive way to reduce heart disease

Juan Mann from Sydney, Australia started a "Free Hug" movement on June 30, 2004. The birth of Free Hug campaign came about when Mann had been feeling depressed and lonely after experiencing some difficult times in his life. Mann was unaware of how something a small as a hug from a complete stranger could make such a big difference in his life. He went to the Pitt Street Mall in Sydney carrying a large sign that said; "FREE HUGS." Juan's campaign involved offering hugs to a total strangers as his random act of kindness hoping to make someone's day a little brighter. His free hug campaign was successful and it continues today. "FREE HUGS" is a month long celebration beginning on the first Saturday of July through the first Saturday in August. This act began the National Hug Day across the globe.

Activities:

- How many words can you make out of the words **National Hug Day**, or see what words you can make with each letter of the National Hug Day. eg.

N ice
A ffectionate
T ouch
I
O
N
A
L
H
U
G
D
A
Y

Or Play Tic-Tac-Toe in groups of 2 having a tournament, each must win the most games out of 10, the winner plays the next until there is a winner. The winner gets a bag of Hershey chocolate.

For the game O= Hugs; X = Kisses

Make an Acrostic using the phrase National Hug Day

N_____

A_____

T_____

I_____

O_____

N_____

A_____

L_____

H_____

U_____

G_____

D_____

A_____

Y_____

FEBRUARY

Theme: Mardi Gras

Decorate with purple, gold and green, Mardi Gras colors. Play Jazz Music

Food:

   • Kings Cakes – Cinnamon pastry decorated with green, purple and yellow sugar. A little plastic baby is put inside the cake after it's cooked. When it is served, tradition says, whoever gets the baby in their piece of cake has to bring the next Kings cake. The celebration lasts through Fat Tuesday, the day before Lent begins.

Crafts:

   • Decorate masks with feathers, jewels, beads, and glitter. Tradition for the Mardi Gras Balls. Or make strands of beads using purple, yellow and green beads.

History:

The roots of Mardi Gras can be traced back to the 17th & 18th centuries to medieval Europe. This tradition passed through Rome and Venice to the French House of the Bourbons and throughout the French colonies. Jean Baptiste Le Moyne Sieur de Bienville, a French-Canadian explorer, discovered a plot of ground 60 miles directly south of New Orleans and named it "Pointe du Mardi Gras. This was on March 2, 1699 and he realized he arrived on the eve of their festive holiday but the celebration did not happen that year. It wasn't until 1703 that Bienville celebrated the very first American Mardi Gras in Mobile where he lived.

Secret Societies, called Masque de la Mobile, were established in 1704 similar to the Mardi Gras krews they have today. This traditions continued until 1709. But in 1710 the "Boeuf Gras Society" took over the parades until 1861. The parades consisted of a large bull's head that was pushed through the streets by 16 men. Later, Rex, a live bull would be draped in white, paraded through the town as a sign that Lent was coming. This parade before Lent was known as Fat Tuesday, because it would be the last day to eat meat until Lent was over. This day is called "Fat Tuesday" even today.

New Orleans was established in 1718 by Bienville and later in the 1730's Mardi Gras became a yearly tradition in New Orleans. Extravagantly decorated floats paraded down the streets while thousands of on-lookers watched. Streets were lined with gaslight torches called "flambeauxs" which added to the festivities. The celebrations didn't stop with the parades. Louisiana's governor, the Marquis de Vaudreuil, incorporated elegant masquerade balls that were attended by wealthy New Orleans residents.

Throughout the years many more crews have been formed creating more and more elaborate floats each year. Each float has a Mardi Gras King and Queen who rides the float in the parade. Each float has beads and doubloons, which are coin-like treasures with the insignia of their float imprinted on them, that they throw to the crowds as they parade by. Zulu crew has a different idea of treasures and throws coconuts from their float as they pass by. The crowds are heard to yell, "throw me something mister" in hopes to get a souvenir bead or doubloon from the event.

Most Mardi Gras crews today are private social clubs with restricted membership policies. Parades and events are funded by its membership, giving the City of New Orleans a spectacular free show.

Activities:

- Surf the Internet for Mardi Gras Trivia and puzzles to enhance your program.
- Dress up with Mardi Gras colors and enjoy a parade. Toss plastic beads from the Dollar Store or other inexpensive trinkets.
- Perhaps you can share a Louisiana style meal of jambalaya or red beans and rice to round out the day's festivities.
- Cajun music might be played in the background and can be easily found on Itunes at a modest cost.
- Have a Mardi Gras mask contest, judging the masks created in the craft mentioned above.

Theme: Ground Hog Day

Display a Pennsylvania Map and locate Punxsutawney. Copy a picture of Punxsutawney Phil to display

Food:

- Assorted nuts or Donuts with nuts, or serve granola on yogurt or Ice cream

Craft:

- Combine the craft and food by making "dirt" - Purchase large can of prepared chocolate pudding, spoon out a small amount into a bowl and add a tablespoon of cool whip and blend until it's all mixed in, put a couple of Oreo cookies in a small ziplock bag and crush with your hands or with the end of a spoon. Now all the ingredients are ready assemble them in a small clear cup. First add the pudding mixture and then crumble the crushed Oreos on top. Make a hole with your spoon in the center of the "dirt" and use Teddy grams cookies or animal cracker to play the part of the groundhog.

History:

Every February 2nd in the United States, a crowd of onlookers wait for that famous groundhog, Punxsutawney Phil, to predict how much longer winter will last. Phil is retrieved from his cage and a large crowd waits in anticipation to see if he will see his shadow or not. Tradition has it that if he sees his shadow, six more weeks of winter are coming. If he doesn't, Spring is just around the corner. Where did this tradition get started you might ask? Let's look at the history and see.

Groundhog day is traced back to an ancient European tradition and is grounded in superstition. While studying the Winter and Spring equinox, early European Christians would celebrate Candlemas, which was 40 days after Christmas, landing on February 2nd. This was the halfway point between Winter and Spring and the farmers used this day to predict the upcoming weather. If the weather was sunny that day, the farmers would expect six more weeks of bad weather, but if the weather was cloudy then Spring was close at hand. This tradition made its way to Germany where they changed the tradition by using a hedgehog as the animal to look for it's shadow. If it saw it's shadow, it meant 6 more weeks of Winter, if not Spring was near.

The Pennsylvania Tradition began in the 1700's when Germans began settling in Pennsylvania and brought this European Tradition with them. Hedgehogs were not as plentiful in the United States so seeing that the groundhogs were plentiful and resembled hedgehogs they were the perfect substitute. The tradition continued and in 1886, the first recorded weather prediction took place by "Punxsutawney Phil. The Pennsylvania paper, the Punxsutawney Spirit recorded the famous groundhog as, "Punxsutawney Phil, Seer of Seers, Sage of Sages, Prognosticator of Prognosticators and Weather Prophet Extraordinary." The United States have been celebrating Groundhogs Day ever since.

Activities:

- Watch the movie Groundhogs Day with Bill Murray & Andie MacDowell if time allows.

- If not, search the Internet for Groundhog Day trivia and facts.
- Invite a local meteorologist to speak about groundhogs and the coming of Spring.

Theme: Chinese New Year

Decorate with the animal of the Chinese year, dragons, and rabbits. Have the participants to wear red.

Food:

- Egg Rolls, fortune cookies, hot and cold tea. Dumplings, and noodles are the traditional foods eaten for Chinese New Years and can also be served. Use chopsticks to eat.

Crafts:

- Get a book to learn how to fold origami cranes and get everyone involved in making them to share.
- Make Chinese lanterns. Search Internet for pattern or Oriental Trading on line for craft kits.

History:

The history of Chinese New year has a number of traditional stories, but the one that Chinese can agree on is Nian. This horrible mythical monster, Nian, preys on the villagers. Nian, who name means year, is a lion-looking monster who comes out on Chinese New Year, which is a 15 day festival. This traditional celebration is enjoyed by 1/6 of the world population and a billion Chinese citizens each year. Chinese New Year is also called Spring Festival or Lunar New Year. Traditional it is celebrated after the second full moon following winter solstice. This celebration goes back to the 12th century when they started using the Western calendar. Originally the celebration was to honor households and heavenly deities and ancestors. The most important part of

Chinese New Year is it brings families together and is viewed as the most important social and economic holiday in China.

China is not the only country who celebrates this holiday. You can experience Chinese New Year in Rome, Paris, London, Jakarta, Sydney and the largest celebration outside of China is found in San Francisco which celebrate with a big parade. This large celebration is due to the influx of Chinese immigrants who migrated to California in the 1840s and 50s looking to get rich during the Gold Rush era.

Each year the celebration features one of the twelve Chinese zodiac animal symbols. And each year a different animal is featured. The twelve animals include a rabbit, dragon, horse, rat, tiger, ox, sheep, monkey, rooster, dog, pig, or snake. These animals are like the zodiac signs used in the United States. Two animals that are particularly important to the Chinese, are the dragons and rabbits. Chinese believe that they are descendants of the dragon, therefore they display dragons as decorations everywhere. They also believe that on the 15th day of the new year, during their Festival of Lanterns, a Chinese goddess, Chang E, took a rabbit with her when she jumped on the moon. This belief is why paper meche' rabbits are displayed everywhere during this holiday.

Another tradition during Chinese New Year is for Chinese families to clean out their homes to get ready for the New Year. The believed is that you need to clean out the house in order to get rid of ghosts and bad luck left from the last year. You may see people getting rid of debt, changing their look for the new year with new clothes and hairdo, and make amends with people they have had disagreements with in the past year. These events are like

American's New Year's resolutions making a fresh start for a better year ahead.

Families wanting good fortune for the year, make dumplings together as a family, late in the evening, as part of their celebration. They also make noodle dishes, but must make sure they don't break the noodles which will interfere with their long life. The final tradition is to wear red for good luck avoiding black which represents death.

Activities:

• Each year in the Chinese zodiac has an animal associated with it. People who are born in that year are said to have the characteristics of the animal of the year. Look up the years for each animal and determine what animal represents each participant. Read the information on each participant's animal. Many Chinese restaurants have placemats with this information printed on them. Call around and you may be able to get enough to share or can get permission to copy and share.

• Learn how to use chopsticks. Have small balls, marbles or items to practice picking up with the chopsticks.

Theme: Ferris Wheel Day

Food:

- Fair Foods like: Funnel Cake, Candy Apples, Corn Dogs, Sodas.

Crafts:

- Popsicle Ferris wheel – You need Popsicle sticks and glue. Search the internet for the photo of this craft under Popsicle Ferris wheel craft.

History:

A beautiful night, colored lights everywhere, the smell of funnel cake and a huge wheel lightening up the sky. The center of this landscape is the beloved Ferris wheel. So where did the story of the Ferris Wheel begin? Well in 1891, America was looking for an impressive structure, like the Eiffel Tower in France, to commemorate the 4th anniversary of Columbus discovering America. A Pennsylvanian engineer, George Washington Gale Ferris, Jr, got to work and created a large wheel designed. To this huge wheel he put seats, lights and music creating an exciting ride that allowed participants of the celebration to see the entire celebration from high above the ground. Fair goers and amusement park attendees know this ride as the Ferris Wheel.

This exhilarating ride made its debut in 1893 at Colombian Exposition in Chicago. The Ferris Wheel was 830 ft in circumference and the radius was approximately 125 ft. Two 140 feet tall steel beams held the wheel in place. The engine needed 2000 horsepower to turn this massive wheel. The height of the wheel was 264 ft high and held 36 seats that could hold 60 passengers each with a grand total per ride was 2160 passengers. The ride time was 20 minutes to complete only 2 rotations of the wheel.

The cost per ride was only 50 cents.

This first Ferris Wheel was only erected twice before it was destroyed by dynamite in 1906. The Ferris Wheel was reproduced in many countries from 1895 – 2008, and the heights ranged from 212 ft high to 541 feet high. Some of the countries you can find them in were UK, Austria, France Japan, London China and Singapore.

Ferris Wheels to center stage at all events, fairs and carnivals until the invention of the roller coaster in 1885.

Activities:

- Look up the first Ferris Wheel Fun Facts to ask the participants.

- Find a video online of a Ferris Wheel ride and play it on a large screen TV. Solicit feelings and comments about what it feels like to ride a Ferris Wheel. Ask what was the largest Ferris Wheel people rode on or about anything special that may have happened while riding a Ferris Wheel.

Theme: Random Acts of Kindness

Decorate with hearts

Food:
- Serve cupcakes and/or heart shaped cookies, hot cocoa, hot tea, and coffee

Crafts:
- Make 6 – 12 cards to give to someone when they are having a bad day.

History:

Anne Herbert, the founder of "Random Acts of Kindness," coined this phrase when she wrote these words on a restaurant place mat in 1982. - *"Practice random kindness and senseless acts of beauty."* Little did Anne know that her words on a place mat that day would have such an impact on those around her and across the world. From the restaurant in Sausalito, California, to bumper stickers to human kindness momentum began to spread like wild fires. Acts of kindness both large and small were happening daily and newspapers across the U.S. were highlighting these kind gestures. Radio stations jumped on the band-wagon challenging people to do random acts of kindness which also made the doer feel good too. The kind acts created a good feeling throughout making others want to enjoy this good feeling.

Many teachers have made a class assignment for their students to help them understand the impact these acts can make on their own life and others lives. Random acts of kindness is a concept that has crossed the world with a positive impact. There have been famous people who have written kindness quotes. Here are some of these quotes:

- *Kindness is a language which the deaf can hear and the and the blind can see. ~Mark Twain*

- *No act of kindness, no matter how small, is ever wasted. ~Aesop*

- *Remember there's no such thing as a small act of kindness. Every act creates a ripple with no logical end. ~Scott Adams*

- *Kind words and actions can seem so small, but their effects are truly endless ~ Author* Unknown

New Zealand started celebrating Random Acts of Kindness day and began a foundation that is now known as an international non-profit organization. Many who participate in this day, have learned how enjoyable doing these acts of kindness are for them as the one who receives the kind act.

This idea isn't entirely new, if you look in the Bible at Matthews gospel you will read many selfless acts that were performed. Mary willingness to birth Jesus, the Good Samaritan who helped a total stranger that had been beaten and left for dead, and the ultimate act of kindness is Jesus' death on the cross for sinners.

Activities:

- Write 12 nice things on a list that you can do to show kindness to someone you come in contact with during your day. For more suggestions about random acts of kindness read Danny Wallace's book, *Random Acts of Kindness: 365 Ways to Make the World a Nicer Place.*

MARCH

Theme: Glen Miller Day

Food:

> • Congealed salad with fruit or vegetables, strawberry short cake, pineapple upside down cake, Oreo and milk. Coffee and tea.

Crafts:

> • Get tin squares for the participants to decorate with buttons, paint or stickers to replicate tin signs.
>
> • Look up tin hole punch craft projects.

History:

Alton Glenn Miller was born in Clarinda, Iowa where he lived for 7 years until his family moved to North Platte, Nebraska. His dad brought home a mandolin one day from work for Miller but Miller was not interested in trying to play a mandolin. Seeing an opportunity to trade the mandolin for a old horn Miller thought his musical career was born. He began to try to learn how to play the horn but playing instruments was not an easy task for Miller and his family wondered if he will ever be a musician.

Miller entered the University of Colorado in 1923 where his career in music started to blossom. He traveled everywhere for auditions and play in many different bands. His busy musical career caused him to neglect his studies and fail several classes. Deciding that music was where his interest lied he dropped out of school to put all his focus on his music career.

This career decision ended up to be a pretty successful choice for Miller, taking him around the United States from Los Angeles to New York. Miller ended up landing a spot in Benny Goodman's orchestra where he was able to write and arrange music too. Having some success, he sent for his college sweetheart, Helen Burger, and they were married. Miller continued to arrange music and play trombone for a living.

Miller's recording career began in 1935 with his record, "Solo Hop," and instrumental arrangement under the Columbia Record recording label. This song reached the top ten on the music charts quickly which was great for his first recording efforts. In 1937 Miller organized a band and was signed to Brunswick records, but this band was not successful and disbanded in 1938. His next job was part of an orchestra that played swing music at the Glen Island Casino in New York. While playing in this band, ten of his songs rose on the hit charts. These songs include: "Sunrise Serenade," "Moonlight Serenade," "Wishing Will Make it So," "Stairway to the Stars," "Moon Love," "Over the Rainbow," "Blue Orchids," and "The Man Wit The Mandolin." Miller was on CBS radio three times a week at that time elevating his popularity, hitting its peak in 1940 as "Tuxedo Junction" sold 115,000 copies the first week of its release followed by another popular hit song, "Pennsylvania 6-5000."

Millers career was going full steam when World War II erupted and Glenn Miller joined the Armed Forces to fulfill his service duty. He was a Captain and had a career leading the USAAF dance band. The sound he created was a great moral booster for the troops abroad, as well as, the families waiting at home. Miller traveled all over entertaining the troops and lifting spirits until a sad event occurred on December 15, 1944. He boarded an aircraft for France for a celebratory concert for liberating the troops in Paris. The aircraft he was on was lost over the English Channel en route to France and was never found.

Activities:

- Listen to the big band music, and have people dance to the music.
- Locate and show the Glen Miller Story, a feature length film, staring Jimmy Stewart.

Theme: History of Kites

Food:

    • Difference shaped crackers, (kite shapes) and cheese. Apple juice, ginger ale, or sparkling wine.

Crafts:

    • Make kites from scratch or assemble a variety of kite kits.

History:

In the year 200 BC, Chinese General Han Hsin of Han Dynasty told his troops to, "go fly a kite," they did and defeated the rebels. Let me explain. They used the kite as a marker for where the wall of the city was. Then they tunneled past the kite which landed them inside the enemy camp for a surprise attack. A pretty ingenious use of a kite wouldn't you say?

Another legend about National Kite Month was when the Chinese would tie a string onto their hats when they were farming so that the wind wouldn't take their hat away and they decided to make structures to attach to strings to fly. This was the first "kite" per say. Seeing hats fly on strings gave them the idea of flying kites. As this idea grew, kites would be use for all kinds of purposes in China and spread to Korea, and across Asia to India cultures. A Buddhist monk introduced the use of kites to Japan as a means of getting rid of evil spirits and to enhance their harvests each year. Flying kites for recreation during the Edo period in Japan exploded so much that the government put a stop to kite flying because they felt it was interfering with work. Some were seen taking breaks to fly their kites.

Sometimes kites were not used for good. The Nagoya Castle, located in the center of Japan, had a thief that used a large kite to lift him to the top of the castle where he proceeded to steal golden statues from the roof. Although he was initially successful, he was later captured and thrown in jail.

Kites were used for love too. An Indian artist in the Mogul Period depicted a lover using a kite to drop notes to his lover who was behind a security wall. Kites were used to carry food way out to sea to feed gar-fish in their feeding areas in Micronesia. Sailors carried kites back as gifts from their service time in Japan and Malaysia in the 16th and 17th centuries, but they didn't have the impact as kites had in other countries.

The 18th and 19th centuries kites were use in scientific research. Benjamin Franklin, Alexander Wilson and others found it to be a helpful tool in learning wind and weather patterns. All this information was helpful in the development of air flight too. This knowledge was used by Sir George Caley, Samuel Langley, Lawrence Hargrave, Alexander Graham Bell, and the Wright Brothers as they worked on their scientific projects. Later kites were used to raise meteorological instruments to track weather in the sky.

A creative teacher in 1822 named George Pocock, used a pair of kites to propel his usually horse-drawn carriage. Pocock was able to travel at 20 miles an hour for 100 miles, even getting out of the "horse toll" since his carriage wasn't being propelled by a horse.

The military found important uses for kites during World War I. Kites carried observation cameras to strategic areas as a means for observing their enemies. They were also used to signal their own troops of danger. Other styles of kites were used for target practice, as a guide for the planes, and recognition for where the sea began.

As scientific discoveries for military strategy continued, kites became obsolete for military jobs and began to be more of a recreational hobby. In the last 50 years, kites have been made with new materials, such as ripstop nylon, fiberglass, and carbon graphite, making kite flying easier and more fun to fly. Many styles, sizes and designs of kites can be found for kite enthusiasts to purchase and enjoy.

Now repeating the famous line from the movie, Mary Poppins, "Let's go Fly a Kite."

Activities:

- Fly the kites made in the craft section.
- Display a large variety of kites.
- Sing, "Let's go Fly a Kite."
- Partner with a local preschool to make and fly kites. Talk about different types of kites: Power Kite, Delta Kite, Sled kite, Box kite, and Winged Box kite. Have pictures of the different type of kites. Talk about their experiences flying kites.

Theme: Dr. Seuss Day

Food:

- Multicolored Goldfish crackers for "One Fish, Two Fish, Red Fish, Blue Fish."
- Layer tall clear glasses with whip cream and strawberries so that they look like the "Cat in the Hat" hat.
- Layer cake with difference colored layers or cupcakes topped with red icing, a marshmallow another red icing to look like the "Cat in the Hat" hat.
- Blue Jello with a Swedish fish in it.

Crafts:

- Two small terracotta flower pots and one pot saucer needed for each participants. Paint the saucer red or white. Take one pot and paint red and white strips going up the pot, so it looks like the "Cat In The Hat's" hat. The saucer will be the hat brim. Paint the other pot black. When the black pot dries glue on a paper printed "Cat in the Hat" face. Next stack the saucer on top of the face pot and then put the striped pot on top of the saucer and then you have a "Cat In The Hat" craft finished.

History:

When you hear the words, "Oh the Places You'll Go" or "I Do Not Like Green Eggs and Ham," there is only one name that comes to mind – Dr. Seuss. Theodor Seuss Geisel was born in Springfield, Massachusetts in 1904. His name sake, German father and grandfather made their living as brew-masters. His mother, Henrietta Seuss

Geisel, was his inspiration for the rhyming style writing Dr. Seuss used in his writings. As a child she would lull her children to sleep with rhymes at bedtime.

Having a comfortable childhood, it all began to crumble as his family experienced the difficulties of World War I. Prohibition changed their easy life-style to a few years of struggles. After the war, life resumed as it was before for their family.

Dr. Seuss studied at Dartmouth College and became the editor-in-chief of the Dartmouth magazine, The Jack-O-Lantern. This position was short lived when he participated in a drinking party, breaking the prohibition law, and school policy. This glitch didn't stop him from writing for the magazine, he just penned his stories under a Penn name of "Seuss," which was his mother's maiden name.

Following graduation, Dr. Seuss followed his dad's dream of being a college professor and went to Oxford University in England. He soon found out that this was not his dream or interest and choose to tour Europe instead. Oxford was not a total loss, he met his first wife, Helen Palmer, also a children's book author.

Returning home to the United States he became the cartoonist for, *The Saturday Evening Post,* and other publications where his career began to take off. A large part of his design work was designing Standard Oil advertisements. This kept him busy for 15 years.

World War II demanded another career change for Dr. Seuss. He then tried his hand at a political cartoon for *PM magazine*. He was unable to enlist due to his age, so he contributed to the U. S. Army by making animated training movies for the troops. He also continued to write and illustrate for *Life, Vanity Fair, Judge* and other magazines.

While contributing to all these publications he was offered a contract with Viking Press to write a children book, *"Boners."* This book was not successful but he got noticed as an illustrator. His first, written and illustrated book took 27 tries before it was published. This book is titled, *"And to Think That I saw It on Mulberry Street."*

After his struggling beginning, Dr. Seuss had an instant hit book, *"The Cat in the Hat."* Using his childhood city as inspiration for his story book pallets he became a successful children writer and illustrator. He used the landscape of the Springfield Forest Park for his *"Horton Hears a Who,"* book. The Sneetches in this book were inspired by the Knox tractor, and a mayor in this stories looks like the Springfield Mayor. His successful career provided 44 wonderful children books which includes; *"Green Eggs and Ham,"* *"Oh, the Places You'll Go,"* *"Fox in Socks,"* and *"How the Grinch Stole Christmas."* This wonderful author provides enjoyment to children all over the world.

Activities:

- Make a photo board for the participants to look like a Dr. Seuss character. You can make a red and white hat, black pipe cleaner whiskers, and big red bow tie. Cut a hole in the board for the participants face and take their picture. Decorate a frame with buttons or fun Dr. Seuss shapes.

- Get some Dr. Seuss books from the library and have the participants read them to the group. Ask participants if they could be any Dr. Seuss character, which would they be and why.

Theme: Alfred Hitchcock Day

Decorate with black birds, from the movie, "The Birds"

Food:

- Make birthday cake (the birds attack during a child's birthday party) or popcorn because it's a movie. Coffee, tea and soda.

Crafts:

- Use a light source and have the participants stand with their profile facing sideways as Alfred Hitchcock did in his movies. Trace around their profile on black construction paper, cut them out and mount on another piece of paper. You can hang them in the hall of the facility to see if others can guess who they are.

History:

Alfred Joseph Hitchcock was the master of suspense movies during the 1920s and 1930s. Born in London he had a rough childhood, with strict, stern parents who sent him to boarding school. Prior to this lonely sad existence in boarding school his dad wanted to teach him a life lesson. At the age of 5, he sent him to the police station with a note that said to lock him up for a period of time. Once that time was over he was sent home with a note that said, this is what happens to people who do bad things. This experience had quite an impact on young Hitchcock along with the boarding schools experiences.

Attending St. Ignatius College he became the first game designer inventing games on maps in his alone time.

He was afraid of authority because of his strict upbringing, so he put all his time and attention into his studies. Hitchcock graduated with an Engineering degree from London County Council School.

After graduation he was employed at W.T. Henley Telegraph Company. He was still a loner, and being bored with his day job, he went to a lot of movies, and took drawing class during the night. These classes helped to built his self-esteem, and he began to be more comfortable and witty at work, which drew people to him. Hitchcock began writing stories with his cleaver twists and began to illustrating them too.

Hitchcock's stories began to be published in, *The Henley,* and he began to pen his name as "Hitch."

This opportunity secured him an adverting illustrator job at the magazine which he enjoyed immensely. After years at the magazine company he saw an ad for a new studio coming to London looking for writers and illustrators. He applied for the job and was hired. This company later became American's Paramount studios. American production companies were seen as superior to the British companies so Hitchcock wanted to get established with an American company.

Hitchcock's first opportunity came when he heard of a possible movie production looking for employees. Being interested in this opportunity, he secured an interview. He read the book and made up mock title cards for his interview. Arriving prepared for the audition for the movie he discovered that the production company changed the movie for the film. His quick thinking made him read the new book, write new title cards, and impressed Inlington Studio which landed him the job. He was moonlighting at another company and within a few months and he was hired as their permanent title card designer at the age of 20.

His self-esteem continued to grow and so did his jobs at the studio. He became the assistant for screenwriting, directing, and set design. Hitchcock's big break came when the director became ill while shooting, *Always Tell Your Wife,* and Hitchcock saved the film by finishing the project for the director. This led him to the opportunity to direct the films, *Number Thirteen,* which ended in a tragedy when the studio had to close without finishing the film. Balcom-Saville-Freedman bought the studio, and kept Hitchcock on as an assistant, and successfully produced *"Woman to Woman."* However, their next film, *The White Shadow,* was a failure and caused the theater to closed again.

Once again the theater opened under the Gainsborough Picture Company where Hitchcock received more experience under a talented German filmmaker. Using his special effect camera lens and angles along with Hitchcock's techniques learned in America, they directed the successful film, *The Blackguard.* This German filmmaker produced a different style of film focusing on darker production including madness, suspense, and betrayal rather than comedy, romance and adventure.

It wasn't until 1925 that Hitchcock got his first solo director position with, *The Pleasure Garden.* For this second film he has an assistant named Alma Reville, who caught his eye and later married. She was also in the film industry and became a partner in his film making efforts. The following year Hitchcock directed, *The Lodger,* which was shelved when the distributing company saw it and didn't like it. This film, Hitchcock made a cameo appearance, added humor and had fewer title cards which the producer didn't like. He was rethinking his career after these roadblocks but hung in there and was pleased when the distributing company for, *The Lodger,* ran short of films and decided to put this film in theaters. To everyone's surprise it was a great success.

Alfred Hitchcock had become a success in his career producing numerous hit films, and his home life was successful too. He and Alma had a daughter, Patricia, and their family was complete. His streak of success included the following films: *The Man Who Knew Too Much, The 39 Steps; Secret Agent, Sabotage, Young and Innocent,* and the *The Lady Vanishes.* His success caught the eye of another American film maker which advanced his career in Britain and America. He also won the New York Critics' Award for the best film in 1938. He was flying high.

Hitchcock enjoyed going to different locations to shoot scenes for his movies, from the domed roof of the British Museum in *Blackmail* and Mt. Rushmore for chase scenes in *North by Northwest,* to the Statue of Liberty for a fall scene in *Saboteur,* to Monte Carlo for a car scene in *To Catch a Thief.* The most famous would be the black birds gathered in a schoolyard in, The *Birds.* His thrillers also had the usual leading ladies, comedy and interesting characters woven into his movies.

Hitchcock not only had a successful movie career, he also had a ten year stretch on TV with his *Alfred Hitchcock Hour* series. He started Shamley Productions which is named after his childhood home town in England. The TV series were written by various featured writers, beginning and ending the show with Hitchcock's famous monologues and his silhouette.

From his humble, insecure, lonely beginnings Hitchcock made his mark by receiving the Irving Thalberg Memorial Award, the Life Achievement Award from the

American Film Institute, and Knighted by Queen Elizabeth II. In 1983 Hitchcock died of kidney failure at the age of 80.

Activities:

- Find-a-Word of Hitchcock films
- Find pictures of Hitchcock film movie posters and create a list of those films. Match the poster with the right movie title and see if participants can remember the story of the film.

Alfred Hitchcock Movies

```
Y  O  F  F  G  P  K  A  X  V  L  C  H  C  M  L  Y  E  N  H
D  C  E  S  R  N  S  T  P  S  Y  C  H  O  X  W  W  N  C  R
Q  Y  I  S  R  E  I  H  H  Q  H  V  I  G  M  O  F  U  J  O
L  L  H  Z  N  L  N  E  C  E  R  Y  J  V  D  V  M  O  D  P
P  D  T  G  Y  J  H  Z  V  L  T  K  S  N  E  O  X  Q  H  E
J  M  A  H  T  U  B  F  Y  K  O  H  I  T  O  O  T  N  Y  R
L  T  H  E  T  R  O  U  B  L  E  W  I  T  H  H  A  R  R  Y
C  M  C  O  K  I  N  L  J  D  R  A  W  R  E  Z  G  U  T  W
G  O  T  G  T  J  M  Y  C  A  J  E  C  L  T  N  C  H  W  Z
E  G  A  T  O  B  A  S  E  V  N  Q  A  K  I  Y  E  T  F  W
I  L  C  R  U  O  Z  R  S  K  S  D  S  R  B  B  N  X  S  P
J  F  O  O  V  E  F  Q  O  R  Y  P  E  T  I  L  W  I  W  Y
O  V  T  K  U  U  I  H  F  V  M  H  E  R  P  E  E  Y  N  U
G  T  U  R  B  B  W  G  A  X  T  D  D  L  M  M  K  Y  T  E
I  C  U  I  E  N  N  N  K  Z  S  S  N  R  L  C  S  L  X  K
T  T  V  F  A  M  I  L  Y  P  L  O  T  A  Y  B  A  M  F  H
R  P  W  M  B  S  S  K  A  D  J  I  C  R  R  I  O  Q  S  J
E  E  E  Z  H  I  Z  I  X  W  X  F  G  C  Q  M  A  U  Z  K
V  H  Q  E  Z  P  F  T  S  G  Z  M  X  X  N  Q  I  C  N  L
T  Z  S  T  B  U  O  D  A  F  O  W  O  D  A  H  S  P  C  D
U  F  J  R  M  L  B  S  N  F  I  I  Q  F  T  C  E  B  W  E
C  E  E  M  Z  P  A  Z  S  A  M  W  O  F  R  A  V  K  Q  V
I  D  T  T  K  C  X  N  S  O  M  D  B  B  L  A  I  W  Q  A
D  T  R  M  I  N  N  Q  C  U  F  G  L  J  W  H  R  D  L  D
I  V  V  K  Y  X  E  S  D  H  I  P  Z  R  V  N  B  B  C  Q
```

FAMILY PLOT	FRENZY	MR AND MRS SMITH
NORTH BY NORTHWEST	PSYCHO	REAR WINDOW
REBECCA	ROPE	SABOTAGE
SHADOW OF A DOUBT	SPELLBOUND	SUSPICION
THE BIRDS	THE LADY VANISHES	THE MAN WHO KNEW TOO MUCH
THE RING	THE THIRTY NINE STEPS	THE TROUBLE WITH HARRY
TO CATCH A THIEF	VERTIGO	

Theme: Peanut Butter and Jelly Day March (2nd)

Food:

- Peanut and jelly sandwiches cut in four pieces.

Crafts:

- Prepare "Mr. Peanut" bodies and let the participants decorate them as "Mr. Peanut" legs, hat, arms, eyes, cane etc.

History:

Can you believe that in 1896, the *Good Housekeeping* Magazine wrote an article about encouraging homemakers to grind up peanuts, spreading it on bread to enjoy a new sandwich called peanut butter? This beloved sandwich that we now pair with jelly was paired with other foods originally. Peanut butter was paired with foods such as pimento cheese or other cheeses, with celery or watercress.

Later that year *Table Talk* magazine introduced the idea that paired jelly with peanut butter. This recipe was a hit in the United States. Julia Davis Chandler was a teacher at the Boston Cooking School of Culinary Science which helped to launch this delicious combination to its popularity it holds today. By the 1920s not only the wealthy were enjoying this recipe, but children were beginning to enjoy bringing this sandwich to school for lunch.

As World War II came about the peanut butter and jelly sandwiches was used as a staple to help sustain the troops during the war. The military learned that this sandwich could go into battle without the need for refrigeration allowing the soldiers to have nutrition to help sustain them on the battlefield. The protein from the peanuts was found to be 27% of needed calories for a healthy diet. It was also learned to have a positive effect on heart health too.

Early in the 20th century, two men, Len Kretchman and David Geske discovered that if you cut the crust off of the sandwich and package it in a sealed container it would last longer. This packaging process was the beginning of providing a way for individuals to carry their favorite sandwich where ever they went. This idea was brought to Smucker's who agreed to join this process and the packaging process was patented. This merger helped the Smucker's Company jelly sales soar. The crustless sandwiches were called Uncrustables. By 2005 the Smucker's Company grew to $60 Million due to the Uncrustables peanut butter and jelly sandwiches.

Today school age children in American consume 1,500 peanut butter and jelly sandwiches by the time they graduate high school. These sandwiches have shown up as a lunch time favorite for the last 50 years. After graduation this peanut butter and jelly sandwich remains a staple for lunches that go into the work place every day.

Activities:

  • Have participants make an acrostic poem using the first letter of

P-E-A-N-U-T B-U-T-T-E-R- A-N-D- J-E-L-L-Y

After the poems have been created have them share their creations with the group.

Acrostic Poem of Peanut Butter and Jelly

P_____

E_____

A_____

N_____

U_____

T_____

B_____

U_____

T_____

T_____

E_____

R_____

A_____

N_____

D_____

J_____

E_____

L_____

L_____

Y_____

APRIL

Theme: William Shakespeare

Food:

- Different teas and scones.

Craft:

- Decorate masks, full or partial masks.

History:

When you think of historic English literature your mind immediately think of William Shakespeare. Known worldwide and imitated, memorized and recited by students and actors alike, William Shakespeare's work has be performed in countless theaters and a variety of venues. His 37 plays and collection of sonnets are frequently quoted in casual conversations too.

Shakespeare was born April 26, 1564 into a family of modest means, but his ability for arranging words on a page was a remarkable talent. In time, his way with words would transform the English language. Born in Stratford-upon-Avon only 100 miles from London's bustling market area. He was number three of a family of eight children. No record of his schooling was found, but it is thought that he would have attended the local grammar school where they taught Latin. This was most likely his foundation for his writing skills.

In 1585 Shakespeare was 18 years old, when he got Anne Hathaway pregnant and quickly married her, even though she was eight years older than him. They had Susanna in May that year, and twins, Hamnet and Judith two years later. Unfortunately, his son died tragically at age 11, but he was blessed to still have his two daughters live long lives. William lived most of his productive year pursuing his writing and acting career in London, while Anne lived in the family home in Stratford. It was not until the end of his life that William returned to his home in Stratford.

Three years after Shakespeare's twins were born he disappeared for seven years – but no one is sure where he was and what he was doing. Many speculated that he was writing, performing, studying and teaching his craft. Another rumor was that he poached deer from a local estate and was afraid of a future in jail. Whatever the reason, he became a very educated man, writing works with much knowledge of European and international affairs which he worked into his writings.

In mid 1590s Shakespeare wrote his most famous plays, "Romeo and Juliet," "A Mid-Summer Night's Dream," "Hamlet," "King Lear," "Macbeth" and "The Tempest." Shakespeare used iambic pentameter, metrical rhyming lines, in all his poetry and plays.

Shakespeare's died on April 23, 1616, and that is the date each year his birthday is celebrated in England on the feast of St. George, the patron saint of England.

Activities:

- Assign part to some of the Shakespeare plays and have members of the group perform it.
- Or just have the participants break up the parts and read the famous speeches.

See second page with Balcony Scene from Romeo and Juliet:

See third page for Macbeth's speech

Romeo and Juliet: **Annotated Balcony Scene, Act 2, Scene 2**

Please see the bottom of the main scene page for more explanatory notes.

Scene II. Capulet's Garden.

[Enter Romeo.]

Romeo.
He jests at scars that never felt a wound.

[Juliet appears above at a window.]

But soft, what light through yonder window breaks?
It is the east and Juliet is the sun!
Arise, fair sun, and kill the envious moon,
Who is already sick and pale with grief
That thou her maid art far more fair than she.
Be not her maid, since she is envious;
Her vestal livery is but sick and green,
And none but fools do wear it. Cast it off.
It is my lady, O, it is my love! (10)
O that she knew she were!
She speaks, yet she says nothing; what of that?
Her eye discourses, I will answer it.
I am too bold: 'tis not to me she speaks.
Two of the fairest stars in all the heaven,
Having some business, do entreat her eyes
To twinkle in their spheres till they return.
What if her eyes were there, they in her head?
The brightness of her cheek would shame those stars,
As daylight doth a lamp. Her eyes in heaven (20)
Would through the airy region stream so bright
That birds would sing and think it were not night.
See how she leans her cheek upon her hand
O that I were a glove upon that hand,
That I might touch that cheek!

Juliet.
Ay me!

Romeo.
She speaks.
O, speak again, bright angel, for thou art
As glorious to this night, being o'er my head,
As is a winged messenger of heaven (30)
Unto the white-upturned wondering eyes
Of mortals that fall back to gaze on him
When he bestrides the lazy-puffing clouds
And sails upon the bosom of the air.

Juliet.
O Romeo, Romeo! wherefore art thou Romeo?
Deny thy father and refuse thy name;
Or, if thou wilt not, be but sworn my love,
And I'll no longer be a Capulet.

Romeo.
[*Aside.*] Shall I hear more, or shall I speak at this?

Juliet.
What's Montague? It is nor hand, nor foot,
Nor arm, nor face, nor any other part
Belonging to a man. O, be some other name.
What's in a name? That which we call a rose
By any other name would smell as sweet;
So Romeo would, were he not Romeo call'd,
Retain that dear perfection which he owes
Without that title. Romeo, doff thy name,
And for that name, which is no part of thee, (50)
Take all myself.

Romeo.
I take thee at thy word.
Call me but love, and I'll be new baptis'd;
Henceforth I never will be Romeo.

Juliet.
What man art thou that, thus bescreened in night,
So stumblest on my counsel?

Romeo.
By a name
I know not how to tell thee who I am:
My name, dear saint, is hateful to myself,
Because it is an enemy to thee. (60)
Had I it written, I would tear the word.

Juliet.
My ears have yet not drunk a hundred words
Of thy tongue's uttering, yet I know the sound.
Art thou not Romeo, and a Montague?

Romeo.
Neither, fair saint, if either thee dislike.

Juliet.
How cam'st thou hither, tell me, and wherefore?
The orchard walls are high and hard to climb,
And the place death, considering who thou art,
If any of my kinsmen find thee here.

Romeo.
With love's light wings did I o'erperch these walls, (70)
For stony limits cannot hold love out,
And what love can do, that dares love attempt:
Therefore thy kinsmen are no stop to me.

Juliet.
If they do see thee, they will murder thee.

Romeo.
Alack, there lies more peril in thine eye
Than twenty of their swords. Look thou but sweet
And I am proof against their enmity.

Juliet.
I would not for the world they saw thee here.

Romeo.
I have night's cloak to hide me from their eyes,
And, but thou love me, let them find me here; (80)
My life were better ended by their hate
Than death prorogued, wanting of thy love.

Juliet.
By whose direction found'st thou out this place?

Romeo.
By love, that first did prompt me to enquire.
He lent me counsel, and I lent him eyes.
I am no pilot, yet, wert thou as far
As that vast shore wash'd with the furthest sea,
I should adventure for such merchandise.

Juliet.
Thou knowest the mask of night is on my face,
Else would a maiden blush bepaint my cheek (90)
For that which thou hast heard me speak tonight.
Fain would I dwell on form; fain, fain deny
What I have spoke. But farewell compliment.
Dost thou love me? I know thou wilt say 'Ay',
And I will take thy word. Yet, if thou swear'st,
Thou mayst prove false. At lovers' perjuries,

They say, Jove laughs. O gentle Romeo,
If thou dost love, pronounce it faithfully:
Or if thou thinkest I am too quickly won,
I'll frown, and be perverse, and say thee nay, (100)
So thou wilt woo: but else, not for the world.
In truth, fair Montague, I am too fond;
And therefore thou mayst think my 'haviour light:
But trust me, gentleman, I'll prove more true
Than those that have more cunning to be strange.
I should have been more strange, I must confess,
But that thou overheard'st, ere I was 'ware,
My true-love passion: therefore pardon me;
And not impute this yielding to light love
Which the dark night hath so discovered. (110)

Romeo.
Lady, by yonder blessed moon I vow,
That tips with silver all these fruit-tree tops --

Juliet.
O, swear not by the moon, the inconstant moon,
That monthly changes in her circled orb,
Lest that thy love prove likewise variable.

Romeo.
What shall I swear by?

Juliet.
Do not swear at all.
Or if thou wilt, swear by thy gracious self,
Which is the god of my idolatry,
And I'll believe thee. (120)

Romeo.
If my heart's dear love --

Juliet.
Well, do not swear: although I joy in thee,
I have no joy of this contract to-night:
It is too rash, too unadvised, too sudden;
Too like the lightning, which doth cease to be
Ere one can say 'It lightens.' Sweet, good night!
This bud of love, by summer's ripening breath,
May prove a beauteous flower when next we meet.
Good night, good night! as sweet repose and rest
Come to thy heart as that within my breast! (130)

Romeo.
O, wilt thou leave me so unsatisfied?

Juliet.
What satisfaction canst thou have to-night?

Romeo.
The exchange of thy love's faithful vow for mine.

Juliet.
I gave thee mine before thou didst request it:
And yet I would it were to give again.

Romeo.
Wouldst thou withdraw it? for what purpose, love?

Juliet.
But to be frank, and give it thee again.
And yet I wish but for the thing I have:
My bounty is as boundless as the sea,
My love as deep; the more I give to thee, (140)
The more I have, for both are infinite.

Nurse calls within

I hear some noise within; dear love, adieu!

Anon, good nurse! Sweet Montague, be true.
Stay but a little, I will come again.

Exit, above.

Romeo.
O blessed, blessed night! I am afeard.
Being in night, all this is but a dream,
Too flattering-sweet to be substantial.

Re-enter JULIET, above.

Juliet.
Three words, dear Romeo, and good night indeed.
If that thy bent of love be honourable,
Thy purpose marriage, send me word tomorrow, (150)
By one that I'll procure to come to thee,
Where and what time thou wilt perform the rite;
And all my fortunes at thy foot I'll lay
And follow thee my lord throughout the world.

Nurse.
[*Within*] Madam!

Juliet.
I come, anon.--But if thou mean'st not well,
I do beseech thee--

Nurse.
[*Within*] Madam!

Juliet.
By and by, I come:--
To cease thy suit, and leave me to my grief: (160)
Tomorrow will I send.

Romeo.
So thrive my soul--

Juliet.
A thousand times good night!

Exit, above.

Romeo.
A thousand times the worse, to want thy light.
Love goes toward love, as schoolboys from
their books,
But love from love, toward school with heavy looks.

Retiring.

Re-enter JULIET, above.

Juliet.
Hist! Romeo, hist! O, for a falconer's voice,
To lure this tassel-gentle back again!
Bondage is hoarse, and may not speak aloud; (170)
Else would I tear the cave where Echo lies,
And make her airy tongue more hoarse than mine,
With repetition of my Romeo's name.

Romeo.
It is my soul that calls upon my name:
How silver-sweet sound lovers' tongues by night,
Like softest music to attending ears!

Juliet.
Romeo!

Romeo.
My dear?

Juliet.
At what o'clock to-morrow
Shall I send to thee? (180)

Romeo.
At the hour of nine.

Juliet.
I will not fail: 'tis twenty years till then.
I have forgot why I did call thee back.

Romeo.
Let me stand here till thou remember it.

Juliet.
I shall forget, to have thee still stand there,
Remembering how I love thy company.

Romeo.
And I'll still stay, to have thee still forget,
Forgetting any other home but this.

Juliet.
'Tis almost morning; I would have thee gone:
And yet no further than a wanton's bird; (190)
Who lets it hop a little from her hand,
Like a poor prisoner in his twisted gyves,
And with a silk thread plucks it back again,
So loving-jealous of his liberty.

Romeo.
I would I were thy bird.

Juliet.
Sweet, so would I:

Yet I should kill thee with much cherishing.
Good night, good night! parting is such sweet sorrow,
That I shall say good night till it be morrow. (200)

Exit above

Romeo.
Sleep dwell upon thine eyes, peace in thy breast!
Would I were sleep and peace, so sweet to rest!
Hence will I to my ghostly father's cell,
His help to crave, and my dear hap to tell.

Exit

MacBeth's Speech

Banquo
All's well.
I dreamt last night of the three weird sisters:
To you they have showed some truth.

Macbeth
I think not of them.
Yet, when we can entreat an hour to serve,
We would spend it in some words upon that business,
If you would grant the time.

Banquo
At your kind'st leisure.

Macbeth
If you shall cleave to my consent, when 'tis,
It shall make honor for you.

Banquo
So I lose none
In seeking to augment it, but still keep
My bosom franchised and allegiance clear,
I shall be counseled.

Macbeth
Good repose the while!

Banquo
Thanks, sir: the like to you!

Exeunt BANQUO and FLEANCE

MacBeth
(*to the SERVANT*) Go bid thy mistress, when my
drink is ready,

She strike upon the bell. Get thee to bed.

Exit Servant

Is this a dagger which I see before me,
The handle toward my hand? Come, let me clutch thee.
I have thee not, and yet I see thee still.
Art thou not, fatal vision, sensible
To feeling as to sight? Or art thou but
A dagger of the mind, a false creation,
Proceeding from the heat-oppressèd brain?
I see thee yet, in form as palpable
As this which now I draw.
Thou marshall'st me the way that I was going,
And such an instrument I was to use.
Mine eyes are made the fools o' th' other senses,
Or else worth all the rest. I see thee still,
And on thy blade and dudgeon gouts of blood,
Which was not so before. There's no such thing.
It is the bloody business which informs
Thus to mine eyes. Now o'er the one half-world
Nature seems dead, and wicked dreams abuse
The curtained sleep. Witchcraft celebrates
Pale Hecate's offerings, and withered murder,
Alarumed by his sentinel, the wolf,
Whose howl's his watch, thus with his stealthy pace,
With Tarquin's ravishing strides, towards his design
Moves like a ghost. Thou sure and firm-set earth,
Hear not my steps, which way they walk, for fear
Thy very stones prate of my whereabout,
And take the present horror from the time,
Which now suits with it. Whiles I threat, he lives.
Words to the heat of deeds too cold breath gives

A bell rings

I go, and it is done. The bell invites me.
Hear it not, Duncan, for it is a knell
That summons thee to heaven or to hell.

Exit

Theme: Barber Shop Quartet Day

Decorate with red and white, straw hats, barbershop poles, and Norman Rockwell's picture of the Barbershop Quartet

Food:

- Strawberries short cake, coffee.

Crafts:

- Have circles, googly eyes, different mustaches, hair and bowties. Make 4 singers as a craft project by gluing the circles on another piece of paper and decorating the faces like a barbershop quartet group. See Pinterest for idea by looking up Barbershop Quartet heads.

History:

Striped jackets, straw hats and mustaches and what comes to mind? - Barbershop quartets. The name came from the fact that music was made while waiting to get your hair cut in the barbershop. The question of where it began is controversial. The 1600's in the barbershops of England, a stringed instrument called a lute, was provided for waiting customers to use to entertain themselves while waiting for a shave and a haircut. Other customers made their instrument by put coins in a candlestick which added a different sound to the music. And voila, barbershop music began.

Another thought about Barbershop Quartets came when immigrants brought their four part harmony in the form of hymns, psalms, and folk songs. Minstrel shows in the 1800s had blackfaced white singers depicting plantation life skits and songs.

Southern black quartets began popping up in American in 1870s. Once they introduced the barbershop harmony, it spread around the world. Performers of this music popped up everywhere due to the introduction of the phonograph by Thomas Edison. Two famous groups who sang this style music are, The American Four, and The Hamtown Students. These groups would harmonize in the barbershops while improvising the words, and every barbershop seemed to have its own group of informal performers.

In the 1930s Barbershop music was in Barbershops all over America. This gathering place was a social club for men in the community to share stories, socialize and create a capella music. Customers began joining in the harmony making beautiful music while they waited for service. By the end of the 19th century the main performers of this style of music were white men.

Later four part harmony sheet music came about and more groups began singing the barbershop style arrangements. The lead singer sang the melody, the tenor sang the harmony, the bass sings the low notes, and baritone completes the sound.

So where did the mustaches, stripped jackets, and straw hats come from? The four men pre-shows entertainers in the Vaudeville show created the fun sounds in front of the curtain prior to the main show. The stripped jackets and straw hats became the customary dress for these pre-show performers and that is why you often times see the Barbershop Quartets dressed in this manner.

Activities:

- Listen to barbershop quartet music.

- Show a clip from The Music Man where a quartet is formed in the movie.

- Bring in a quartet group to sing a few numbers.

Theme: National Humor Month

Food:

- Make Minion cupcakes, coffee and tea.
- Another option is to cut 2 slice of red apples for the lips and put peanut butter to hold small marshmallows in between the two small slices for teeth. This option will resemble our mouth where we smile, laugh, and tell jokes. It also would be a healthy snack.

Crafts:

- Paint flat rocks different colors, and decorate them with googly eyes and a smile. You can use pom-poms for hair. They can be put in their rooms to remind them to laugh every day. For more ideas search "monster rocks" on the Internet for other design ideas.

History:

"A Cheerful heart is good medicine, but a crushed spirit dries up the bones," is good advise found in Proverbs 17:22. Larry Wile, a bestselling humorist knows and practices this advise daily. The founder of National Humor Month, Wilde decided in 1976 to share his findings with the world by establishing National Humor Month. In fact Wilde shares his secrets how to incorporating humor in your daily life in his many books and through speaking engagements to Corporate America.

Wilde chose April as National Humor month because everyone is feeling down about having to pay taxes, so he thought why not change the focus to something positive.

Besides the month already begins with April Fools Day so why not carry on the laughter throughout the whole month.

In addition to sharing a few laughs, just the act of laughing is physically and physiologically great for the body and soul. Like other forms of exercise, laughter increases your blood flow, increases your heart rate allowing more oxygen to be delivered to your body's tissues. Laughter lifts one's spirits instantly, and burns calories. Research shows laughter has healing powers along with reducing stress and fatigue. All these benefits without taking any pills - hence laughter is "good medicine." Scientist, Norman Cousins says that laughter is like an internal jog to the body.

Although humor is good medicine, it is also very personal. What may be funny to one person will not have the same reaction to another. There are cultural differences with humor as well, so you must choose your jokes and pranks wisely in order to get the desired response from your audience.

Wilde has five "must do's" for individuals to add humor to their lives. **The first is to learn to laugh out loud.** Laughter restores the blood pressure, restores the bodies chemical balance, oxygenates the blood, stimulates circulation, aides digestion, relaxes the bodies systems, and messages the vital organs. A good belly laugh is the answer to this step.

His second advice is to, **learn to laugh at yourself.** If you are able to laugh at yourself it shows that you are secure and have high self-esteem. Looking at a situation and being able to find the humor in something you did, and being comfortable enough to laugh about it is a very positive activity.

Wilde's third step is to, **acquire a taste for things that are funny.** Look around the world there are funny things everywhere. Read signs as you drive about town. I once saw a sign at a dry cleaners that said, *"Drop your pants here."* Now we know that they wanted you to use their dry cleaning service, but to read it as a literal statement, it's quite funny. Or another sign I saw for a Weight Watcher meeting location displayed under a 70's clothing store named, *"A Little Bit Hippie."* Now that is funny. Stay alert as you go through our world and you will find many humorous things.

The fourth step is to, **expose yourself to something funny every day.** People who are not in this mode of thinking funny, don't look for the funny things in the world. People are fun to watch, we do and say funny things every day. Sometimes our style of dress can look funny. My husband is a ventriloquist and we often see people who would make a good ventriloquist character for his shows. Look around you and you will begin to see humor too.

Wilde's final step is to **try to see the funny side of life in situations.** Sometimes even the most mundane things we do can turn out comical. I am one who never gets in the right line at the check-out. So instead of raising your blood pressure seething at the checker or the customer in front of you, just think of how ridiculous they are for what antics they go through just to purchase their items. This act of patience will be good medicine and will have better effects for your health.

Stress has the most damaging effect on our health in today's society, but a little laughter each day can do a world of good to reduce bad effects on your mind and body.

Activities:

• Search the Internet for, "Humor for Lexophiles" for a list of funny sayings. Share them and laugh together.

• Find jokes to share with the group.

• Let the participants share good clean jokes they know and give a prize for the best one.

Theme: Winnie the Pooh Day

Food:

- Biscuits and Honey and Tea.

Crafts:

- Book Marker - Copy Winnie the Pooh outlines that you can find online and have the participants color them and put them on a strip of poster board cut in 2" x 6" pieces paper. Then cover the entire project with clear contact paper. The end product is a book marker.

- Make Honey pots. (search Internet for "honey pot" crafts.) Use small mason jars, paint the jars brown leaving the top unpainted. When the brown paint dries, paint the top edge yellow as if the honey was spilling over the top. When both dries tie brown twine around the top for decoration, and then put a sign on the jar that says, "HUNNY." Then the participants can use the jar to keep things in.

History:

The story of Winnie the Pooh began with a real bear story. A lieutenant named Harry Colebourn, was part of a Canadian Infantry Brigade who was being transported to Europe by way of Eastern Canada by train. This was during the First World War. When the train stopped at White River, Ontario, Colebourn purchased a black bear cub from a hunter who had killed it's mother. The bear cost him $20 and he decided to name it Winnipeg after his home town. Later he shortened its name to Winnie.

Winnie became the mascot for the unit and went everywhere with the unit. As time went on Colebourn became Captian of the unit and when the unit was deployed to France to continue the battle, Colebourn presented the bear to the London Zoo. This event happened in 1919, which gave the bear a stable home. Winnie became a major attraction for the zoo and she lived a pampered life until 1934 when she died.

The story continues when A.A. Milne, a famous author, took his son, Christopher Robin, to the London Zoo. Christopher was attracted to Winnie's exhibit and was allowed to spend time inside the cage with the bear too. Christopher loved the bear so much that he named his stuffed teddy bear, Winnie the Pooh. Prior to knowing Winnie, Christopher called his stuffed bear Edward Bear. The Pooh part of the name came from a swan that lived on a pond at Christopher's 100 acre woods where he lived.

When Christopher was little, his father, A.A. Milne, began writing the Winnie the Pooh series of children's books. The boy in the story was of course his son, Christopher Robin. All of Christopher's friends in the stories were created from his childhood stuffed animals. These friends include Eeyore, Piglet, Tigger, Kanga and Roo. Two of his friends are based on animals in his woods at his 100 acres woods home - Rabbit and Owl. This beautiful 100 acre farm is Ashdown Forest in Sussex.

Methuen publishers released Milne's first book, *Winnie The Pooh*, in the fall of 1926. And the second book, *Now We Are Six*, published in 1927, and *The House at Pooh Corner*, the following year. Milne was becoming popular and Winnie the Pooh was becoming a beloved character to children and parents who read these stories. The popularity grew as the books were translated into almost every known language. In 1996 over 20 million copies were sold.

Pooh wasn't just popular with children and families, he gained the attention of Walt Disney's daughter. Her love for the cuddly bear was the push for Walt Disney to incorporate this character into his cast if characters at his amusement parks and to feature Pooh in his films. In 1977 Walt Disney released a film series, *The Many Adventures of Winnie the Pooh*. Winnie the Pooh's popularity grew, and is second only to Mickey Mouse. Two other Pooh films release were, *The Bear of Very Little Brain*, and *Pooh's Grand Adventure*. In 2000 another Winnie the Pooh film was released, but this time the main character was his bouncy friend, Tigger. This movie was called, *The Tigger Movie*.

Activities:

- Word Search of the Winnie the Pooh Characters
- Have a contest to see who can do the best impression of a Winnie the Pooh character.

Winnie The Pooh Characters

```
C  G  S  Y  O  X  V  T  A  I  A  Q  I  M  L  Q  S  N  L  G
O  H  D  P  Y  D  I  A  R  Q  H  F  H  R  O  O  R  O  F  F
P  T  R  X  M  G  N  Q  A  F  I  D  S  A  T  C  A  A  Y  S
W  O  W  I  G  U  S  S  S  E  Q  B  B  B  F  I  L  R  G  R
I  F  R  E  S  O  L  E  Y  A  O  C  C  B  R  M  U  W  F  Z
N  U  R  M  A  T  L  A  E  U  U  P  W  I  H  S  G  Y  R  O
N  C  P  N  L  Z  O  D  F  E  M  G  R  T  P  V  A  F  C  U
I  J  O  G  O  T  L  P  R  F  Y  H  X  L  O  Z  J  R  O  B
E  D  Q  O  S  S  R  T  H  J  E  O  A  G  N  A  K  I  P  W
T  O  W  D  V  J  U  K  K  E  T  H  R  Q  H  L  I  G  N  Q
H  A  M  E  A  T  D  B  Z  H  R  C  L  E  Z  Q  F  J  W  L
E  O  E  D  I  Y  S  X  E  R  M  R  R  L  W  L  K  T  U  O
P  B  S  F  P  Q  F  B  R  M  K  W  O  G  Q  R  H  R  K  Q
O  W  U  T  Q  P  A  I  B  C  L  O  Z  B  X  K  J  O  K  O
O  E  O  P  T  C  O  X  F  C  W  A  A  O  I  C  K  C  S  Q
H  X  N  C  K  Y  T  R  E  B  O  R  E  L  C  N  U  Y  R  Z
I  R  A  S  R  K  K  H  N  H  Q  O  Z  L  O  X  S  H  R  W
F  V  O  R  F  S  G  G  H  H  L  F  R  D  W  M  W  B  R  P
C  N  S  T  L  O  O  V  P  B  K  L  J  H  M  F  R  W  H  I
S  P  K  I  R  N  P  I  G  L  E  T  A  M  O  G  B  Z  G  T
```

BEE	CHRISTOPHER ROBINS	EEYORE
HEFFALUMPS	JAGULARS	KANGA
OWL	PIGLET	RABBIT
ROO	THE BACKSONS	TIGGER
UNCLE ROBERT	WINNIE THE POOH	WOOZLES

MAY

Theme: Horse Racing

Decorate with roses, black-eyed Susans, White Carnations - each race has a different color of flowers.

Food:

Virgin Mint Julep serves 8 – 10 Prep time: 10 min
1 large bunch of mint leaves½ cup sugar
1 bottle of ginger ale (1 liter)½ cup water
1 cup fresh lemon juice crushed ice
Mix and serve

Cucumber Dill Dip: 16 servings
2 – 8oz package of cream cheese room temperature
2 TB chopped fresh dill
1 cup sour cream
½ tsp minced garlic
2 TB finely chopped green onion
2 TB milk
½ tsp salt
1 cucumber diced in small cubes

In a medium bowl, blend cream cheese and sour cream with an electric mixer until smooth. Mix in green onions, cucumbers, salt, dill and garlic. Refrigerate at least 30 minutes to blend flavors. If the dip is too thick add milk, 1 TB at a time until it reaches the consistency that you want it.

**Serve over small slices of bread and put a piece of watercress on top for decoration

Wings: with BBQ sauce not hot sauce and/or Ham biscuits.

Craft:

- Decorate hats to wear to the "Horse Race" with flowers, netting, ribbon, or other decorative items.

History:

Of all the sports around that people enjoy viewing, horse racing is by far the most complex. Breeding the horse, breaking the horse for riding, training the horse for the track, training the horse to stand and respond to the bell in order to dart from the gate at the appropriate time, training the jockey, and learning how the horse responds to the jockey's commands and the other horses on the track are just the beginning to this sport. All these aspects are time consuming, expensive, and necessary for a successfully trained and winning horse.

A winning race horse begins with breeding. Winners need both speed and endurance. The modern sport of horse racing began in earnest back in the 12th century when fast Arabian horses were bred with English mares known more for strength and endurance. The result was a horse that had the best characteristics of both horses.

To say horse racing is big business is an understatement. Owners will spend millions of dollars to obtain a horse with the right pedigree in the hopes of posessing a horse with speed, strength, and endurance. A Triple Crown winner, such as Sea Biscuit, will return the investment many times over. Not only is there prize money for the winners, but product endorsements and appearance fees. Even after the racing years are over, a winning horse will spin off a fortune in breeding fees.

Champion horses do not just show up at the race track. An extensive training process exists for both horse and driver. Yearlings, horses between ages one and two, begin their training process. This is the process called "breaking" the horse, which involves use of a bridle on a lead line and trotting them around in a paddock. As the horse gets comfortable with the bridle, a saddle is added to their backs to get the horse use to having something on their back. When the horse feels comfortable with the saddle, they are ready for the next step, the rider. And finally, they are put in the gate and practiced darting from the gate when the bell rings. This process is called "gate school."

The training schedules of each horse is also meticulously kept, so that they don't progress before they are ready for the next step. This allows the horse not to injure themselves which would be detrimental to their career. The process and progress journal is also a great record for the buyer, so they can know the training process, before they purchase the horse to race. When and if the horse is ready, they are put on the track for their first race.

The third part of this complicated sport is the jockey training. Jockeys begin very young riding horses and even work at stables to get use to handling horses. They must work out to become strong and to build their stamina, to avoid the many injuries that they can easily encounter as a jockey. Some jockeys attend a 2 year college program that trains aspiring jockeys. Jockeys must be in tune with the horse, and must be aware of the other horses on the track, to have a successful career. There is a lot depending on the jockey, so their responsibilities are great to have a successful race. Horse owners depend on the jockeys for their livelihood, and to have a successful horse racing business.

The last step of the process is the actual horse race. Several horse racing tracks are around the United States. The audiences are people who like to go to the tracks to bet on their favorite horse, and see them run the track, and hopefully win the race. The three major horse races that most horse owners would like to win are, the Kentucky Derby, Preakness Stakes, and Belmont Stakes. If the same horse wins all three races they are called the Triple Crown winner. Spectators of horse racing enjoy placing a bet on their favorite horse, in hopes that they come in first, so they can win money off their bet. Other spectators are just as happy watching the horses run the track to see who wins without placing a bet.

Race tracks serve a menu of Cucumber Grenadine dip on bread rounds with watercress on the top, ham biscuits, BBQ wings, "pigs in a blanket," beer, and the famous Mint Juleps.

Activities:

- Horse racing game – You can go on line to purchase a Horse racing game or you can make it with these directions. You can use felt, or poster board and make a six lane straight track. Have each lane broken up into 25 spaces to advance the horses, step by step, to the finish line, which is labeled at the end of the lanes. Purchase six toy horses, one for each lane. Number each lane 1 – 6, and number each horse 1 – 6. You need a set of small or large dice. One dice is used to tell you which horse to move, and the other dice is to tell you how many moves to advance that horse. The horse that gets to the finish line first wins. You can also give each resident chips to bet on their horse.

- Another option may be to show the recent Disney movie, "Secretariat".

Theme: Cartoon Art Appreciation Week - May (18 – 26)

Food:

- Cupcakes made with faces on them.

Crafts:

- Have participants create their own cartoon.

History:

Cartoon drawings and fun captions are nothing new. Cavemen would draw with charcoal or paint on rocks to tell stories in their time. Stick figures of animals, people dancing, or hunting, and depictions of cultural rituals, where recorded in this manner to pass along information to future generations.

Early civilizations such as the Mayans, used cartooning to depict people and events. Hieroglyphics, seen by Egyptian people, were carved into stones and rock walls to tell stories too. As the time went on, different mediums, such as clay and wood were used to tell stories passing along cultural rituals to the next generations. Archaeologist examine these carvings and sculptures to find out about earlier civilizations.

Monks were known to use bright bold colors, to paint pictures as seen in their illustrated Bible stories. (find an example if you can). Cartoon type characters were used in their stories in a caricature style of painting. Some of the early cartoonists were influenced by the Fresco paintings, and sculptures of the 15th and 16th century were used as well.

Benjamin Franklin created the first cartoon as we know them in the year 1754. He was trying to encourage the different states to join the union in this cartoon. His cartoon was a dissected snake that states "Join, or Die." (find a copy of the cartoon). As time went on through the 17th to 19th centuries cartooning moved to more printed mediums like newspapers, and magazines. Cartoonists were also known to illustrate stories and books in a more cartoon type style. The 20th century continued with newspaper political satire and comics - this genra continued to grow. By mid-century, animated films and animated characters mixed with actors, to produce films. Some of these movies were "Mary Poppins" and "Who Framed Roger Rabbit." The mixture of actors and cartoons opened up a larger set of possibilities for film makers and cartoonists.

Some familiar cartoonists include Walt Disney, who brought us the famous character – Mickey Mouse. He also created a whole family of adorable characters that we enjoy seeing in print and in movies. Charles M. Schulz is another familiar cartoonist who created loveable characters and cartoon TV films. The most beloved character he created is Charlie Brown and his sidekick dog, Snoopy.

Another popular cartoonist that has created many children books, filled with characters kids and grown-ups love, is Dr. Seuss. Whether it's "Cat in the Hat," "Green Eggs and Ham," or "Hop on Pop," Dr. Seuss helped kids develop the love of reading because of his whimsical creative characters and stories.

Cartoonists do not limit their work to projects for children. Gary Larson, the creator of Far Side, has been successful in creating his cartoons for adults in 17 languages. Calvin and Hobbes was created by another creative artist, Bill Watterson. His popular characters show up in his 23 million published books. An asthmatic child, Tom Ryan spent much time indoors as a child and used his imagination to create characters and stories. This time spent inside as a child helped him become the creator of the cartoon "Tumbleweeds." He later created that cynical, lazy, lasagna loving cat "Garfield." This fat cat showed up in 41 papers, and grew to millions of readers enjoying his antics.

These cartoonists are just a few wonderful people who make us laugh at normal life events, and they are able to use humorous twists to give the reader a good laugh.

Activities:

- Look up on the Internet how to draw your favorite character such as Charlie Brown, Snoopy, Garfield or others.
- Obtain some cartoons from some of these characters to have for the participants to enjoy.
- Recruit a talented caricature artist to do a caricature of participants.

Theme: International Jazz Day

Food:

- Decadent desserts, coffee and tea.

Crafts:

- Get 2 small aluminum pie pans and punch holes around the edges so they can be tied together. Face the two tins together allowing them to hold beans in the center. Place about 10 or so beans in the pans and tie the two pans together with string or yarn. When they are finished they will make tambourine-shaped shakers for the jazz band.

History:

When you think of Jazz the first artist that comes to mind is Louis Armstrong. This trumpeter, bandleader, and singer was popular among grown-ups and kids alike. In his early years he was a friend to every kid in his neighborhood. You would often see him sitting on his front steps for hours playing his horn and letting them play their horns for him. Although his childhood was troubled, you would never have known that by the way he loved and encouraged the children in his neighborhood.

Armstrong's young life was sad. His dad left his mom when he was born, so his mom worked as a maid. Later he lived with his grandmother because his mother turned to prostitution. While he was a young child, you would often find him performing on the streets for change from passer- by's. While his life as a boy was difficult, he remained positive as he played and wrote beautiful music. He was forced to leave school in the 5th grade to help support the family and was given a job collecting junk and delivering coal for the Karnofsky family. They were kind to him, often feeding him his meals too. Although Armstrong's life was not easy ,he played a major role in the birth of Jazz in this country. In fact his famous song, *"What a Wonderful World,"* was reminiscent of his good times watching the children in his neighborhood grow up.

For over 100 years jazz can be traced back in the United States as part of the African American genera of music. In the 20th century as New Orleans experienced a cultural blending of people, they also experienced a blending of music. This blending of sounds resulting in several popular types of musical sounds being born like Ragtime, Blues, Bebop, Big Band and Jazz. But the Jazz roots can also be traced back to the time of slaves singing work songs. These songs depicted life struggles, and religious beliefs which were the foundational roots of jazz.

Looking for better opportunities, African Americans began moving to Chicago and New York taking the New Orleans Jazz music with them. Radio stations, and dance halls began playing Jazz and Blues for their entertainment. Jazz bands started playing in clubs for people to enjoy and dance to. Girls began to change their look and style by bobbing their hair and wearing short flapper dresses. (get photos of a flapper girls hair and dress to share). Jazz records were produced and purchased by everyone to enjoy in their homes. Jazz was everywhere.

As the 30's came along, new Big Band style Jazz came into the music world. Swing dance with the upbeat dance style music became popular, and jazz took a back seat. Then WWII came along and took many of the African Americans individuals who sang and played in the jazz bands leaving dance halls wanting for singers and musicians to share this sound.

After the war, television came on the scene and became the means for entertainment, so music of all types became second to TV shows entertainment. But shows like, *American Band Stand,* also was born allowing families to enjoy the new musical sounds in the comfort of their own home. *American Band Stand* aired from 1952 through 1969 and turned the music worlds direction to Rock and Roll. Later in 1971 – 2006, another musical TV show came along, *Soul Train.* This show catered to the African American influenced style music which included R&B, soul, disco, hip hop, funk gospel and of course jazz. Jazz was back on the scene.

The civil rights movement in the 60's reintroduced jazz and it came to life becoming more popular than before. As time continued on, Jazz has taken on many forms from acid jazz to smooth jazz. Schools teach jazz sounds in their band programs, orchestras have jazz pieces in their repertoire, and some clubs feature jazz music for your listening pleasure. You will find the most concentrated amounts of jazz music in New Orleans and Chicago featuring all types of jazz. New Orleans funerals still have trumpet, trombone, and saxophone players as the mourners parading along the funeral route dancing and playing jazz music on the way to the cemetery.

If you want to lift your spirits, relax or have wonderful background music for a party, try some jazz and your will see the mood be lifted.

Activities:

- Listen to Jazz music by Louis Armstrong and other jazz artists.
- Look at the words from Louis Armstrong's song, "It's A Wonderful World" and have someone read the or sing the song together.

It's a Wonderful World
I see trees of green, red roses, too,
I see them bloom, for me and you
And I think to myself
What a wonderful world.
I see skies of blue, and clouds of white,
The bright blessed day, the dark sacred night
And I think to myself
What a wonderful world.
The colors of the rainbow, so pretty in the sky,
Are also on the faces of people going by.
I see friends shaking hands, sayin', "How do you do?"
They're really sayin', "I love you."
I hear babies cryin'. I watch them grow.
They'll learn much more than I'll ever know
And I think to myself
What a wonderful world
Yes, I think to myself
What a wonderful world

- Find a local jazz band to entertain

Theme: Cinco De Mayo

Decorate with big Mexican hats, sarape, pinatas, fake peppers

Food:

- Taco's, and/or seven layer bean dip and chips.
- Chips and salsa and/or cheese dip.
- Mock Margaritas.

Crafts:

- This project can be started the week of or before this program because it is a multi-step project. Making a pinata: get 2 cups of flour, 2 cups of water and tablespoon of salt and mix it together. Take newspapers and cut or tear into strips. Get the shape of what you are trying to make either a blown up balloon, or box etc. Then cover the object with the newspaper strips that have been dipped into the flour, salt and water mixture. Look on the internet for ideas for shapes and projects. If you want to make it simple, you can make bee hives out of blown up balloons. Have the top layer covered with yellow tissue paper. Or put wings on it, and put yellow an black stripes around it and make a bee. Or make it red an add a little head formed out of the newspapers and mixture and make a lady bug. You can also paint on the dried form to create the stripes or colors for the characters that you are creating. This project will take overnight to dry. Square boxes could be cakes, house or Sponge Bob cartoon character.

- Another craft could be to make large tissue paper flowers. You take 5 sheets of tissue paper colors that you like, but not more than 7 sheets. Fold them in half long ways and cut down the fold. Then stack the colors how you would like them to show up in your flower, (ex. All yellow in the center and red on the outside, or alternated them) Then stack them all together and start folding all the sheets up about one inch, then flip it over and fold the next fold one inch in the other direction making it look like a fan. Do this all the way up until you have an accordion pleated stack of tissue paper. Take a pipe cleaner and twist around the center of the folded tissue paper. It will fan out when you do this. Next separate each sheet of tissue paper pulling it gently to the center towards the twisted pipe cleaner. Once all the tissue paper is separated and pulled to the center you will have a beautiful mariachi flower. For a You Tube demonstration look up "tissue paper flower" on the Internet.

History:

Cinco de Mayo, celebrated May 5th is not a celebration for Mexico's independence which is actually September 16th. The history behind this celebration started in 1862 in Peublo. Mexican's president, Benito Juarez, declared their country was too poor to pay their international trade debts which stirred up France to come, attack, and try to claim the land. But when they came, a civilian organized army didn't want to lose their control and their land so they fought and won. This win was surprising since they were outnumbered 2 to 1. This became a victory against French Imperialism and the Mexicans were able to beat France , reclaiming and keeping their land. This battle is known as the Franco-MexicanWar. The United States offered to help Mexico over throw any kind of French rule making them our allies. After the war, President Moreze was returned to power.

The United States was impressed with Mexico's ability to regain their power and used their method for tactics in our Civil War. As this feeling of power regained, United States started celebrating Cinco de Mayo too. Parties, parades, mariachi music and folk dance performers filled the street festivals. Margaritas became the signature drink for the celebration. In fact this celebration has grown so much in the United States that this celebration is a bigger in America than in Mexico or in Pubelo where this original event took place. American's do enjoy a good reason to party.

Activities:

- You could have a participants to move "dance" to mariachi music.
- Find a DVD of mariachi bands and Mexican folk dancers to watch.
- Make salsa to enjoy

JUNE

Theme: Oscar the Grouch Day

Food:

- Have participants make sundaes, one of Oscar's favorite foods. Have Swedish Fish and bananas to add to the ice cream which is also how Oscar likes it.

Crafts:

- Get socks, pom poms, googly eyes of various sizes, feathers, fabric squares or anything that could be used to dress a sock puppet.

History:

If you are green, live in a trash can and like to collect trash you must be one of the Sesame Street Characters – Oscar the Grouch. Oscar the Grouch is one of the 14 characters in the show loved by kids and adults around the world. His big eyes, football shaped face and no visible nose, is a fun addition to the repertoire of characters seen on Sesame Street. The character of Oscar is performed by Caroll Spinney.

Jim Henson, the creator of the Sesame Street crew of delightful puppets, began in New York and ran from 1969 – 2000. Oscar was created by Henson and Jon Stone after being served by a horrifically rude waiter. Oscar's puppeteer, Caroll Spinney got the voice from a New York Taxi driver she met. There are two stories about how his name came about. One story is that he was named after a famous restaurant, Oscar's Tavern. The other suggested naming was that Oscar is named after a Canadian folk musician, Oscar Brand since he was an early board member for the Children's Television Workshop. The second story came about when Oscar Brand's 90th birthday was celebrated at the television station.

The original Oscar was created by John Lovelady, and it featured orange fur and one eyebrow.

Oscar is always seen in his trashcan house. His residence is furnished with swimming pool, ice-rink, bowling alley, a farm and a piano. The center of his home has a spiral staircase. The rest of his trash can has trash. Two other pets that have been in Oscars home is his pet worm and elephant.

As time went on, other "grouches" were written into the stories with Oscar. The first movie with the group of grouches was, *The Adventures of Elmo in Grouchland*. Each episode of Sesame Street began with Big Bird, the big yellow bird, interacting with Oscar. Oscar loved to prank people and his favorite was to put catsup in Big Bird's alarm clock.

It's tricky when Big Bird and Oscar are in a scene together. They have to put the voices to Spinney while Jim Martin and Matt Vogel are both needed to manipulate the large puppets. These operation of these puppets to create a flawless performance takes a lot of coordination among the staff.

The second season, Henson took Oscar apart to make it easier for the puppeteers to switched hands during performances. Oscar also took on a new look having his orange fur replaced with the well known green fur.

The Oscar character was to demonstrate diversity of race and ethnic backgrounds. The hope was to promote inclusion of all social economic levels, racial and cultural differences but some saw it as a look at the poor and urban Americans in our country. Later the trash man Bruno made it possible for Oscar to move around town and see other parts of the town. However, Bruno hasn't been on the show for ten years so Oscar hasn't been able to travel about as before.

Earlier shows had Oscar legs coming from the bottom of the trashcan allowing him to dance, walk, and skate. He also left Sesame Street to go to the annual "Grouch Convention." He would also be seen interacting with his orange worm friend, Slimey. They would talk about how Oscar doesn't like anything or anybody but little people and adult Sesame Street fans. The character on the show that Oscar does like is Maria, but he refuses to let her know.

The character of Oscar is wanting to be a big grouch with everyone, but in some episodes of the show you see him replacing Ernie's rubber duck, he hunted for Big Bird when he was lost on Christmas Eve and has shown other acts of kindness to the characters on Sesame Street.

If you want to make friends with Oscar bring him a spinach sardine chocolate fudge sundaes, or mashed bananas with ice cubes and cold beef gravy and you will have a friend forever.

Activities:
- Seek a word of Sesame Characters.

Sesame Street Characters

```
T  X  M  G  X  X  Z  M  T  X  S  F  G  D  C
R  Z  R  I  Y  T  Y  U  Y  G  R  D  R  T  O
E  J  V  M  N  L  O  P  H  H  T  E  N  U  O
B  W  T  C  P  F  L  P  Z  A  H  U  V  B  K
O  S  C  A  R  T  H  E  G  R  O  U  C  H  I
C  I  D  F  G  S  I  T  T  C  S  X  P  Y  E
Z  D  S  D  Y  R  L  E  W  G  S  N  E  M
O  P  R  T  Y  L  O  H  G  A  J  R  S  L  O
D  P  E  E  M  K  T  V  M  C  O  G  T  I  N
O  B  I  G  B  I  R  D  E  S  T  B  F  M  S
T  Q  B  R  L  Q  B  U  I  R  O  Q  P  S  T
G  O  R  F  E  H  T  T  I  M  R  E  K  Y  E
E  I  N  R  E  F  A  T  L  A  Z  O  E  U  R
A  K  X  M  D  N  C  E  O  G  L  Z  H  G  B
N  T  G  M  I  Y  Z  W  S  N  M  A  T  K  B
```

BERT	BIG BIRD	COOKIE MONSTER
ELMO	ERNIE	GROVER
GUY SMILEY	KERMIT THE FROG	MUPPET
OSCAR THE GROUCH	ROSITA	TELLY
THE COUNT	ZOE	

Theme: "Donut" Day

Food:

- Donuts (naturally), coffee, tea and milk

Crafts:

- Use polymer clay that will harden to form a doughnut. The polymer clay comes in different colors as do donuts. Then take other colors of clay for icing, sprinkles or filling. When you finish the donut, it can be displayed on a small plastic plate.

History:

The first Friday of June every year is designated as National Donut Day. A nice benefit is that most donut stores offer patrons a free donut that day. This practice began in 1938 by the Salvation Army as a way to honored the soldiers during War War I. This cake like batter that was fried and topped with sugar glaze, cinnamon or confectionery sugar adds to the enjoyment to those who are consuming them.

Let's go back to see where this practice began. Dr. Morgan Pett, a military physician who was headed to take care of soldiers, decided to stop and pick up 8 dozen donuts to share with the patients after their exam. Pett paired his services with the donut for each patient that day, starting a movement for our service men and women that continues today. One of his patients that day was a Lieutenant General, Samuel Geary, who was so impressed with the idea of pairing a donut with their appointment, prompted him to decide to do fund raisers to make sure this practice continued every day for every patient. His efforts were a great success and continued to be practiced by Dr. Pett.

Later this practice was supported by the Salvation Army. The Salvation Army sent 250 volunteers to France, set up "huts" as canteens/social gathering places along the war zones that would provide a number of services as well as donuts. Besides donuts, mending, writing supplies, and other baked goods were served and these canteens served as a place for soldiers to socialize. The women who provided these services in 1918 were known as "Donut Dollies." The title "doughboys" for the infantry in WWI came from the introduction of these donuts and socializing huts into their daily lives.

The beginning of donuts for patients continues today. Chicago still has donut fundraisers for the Salvation Army to distribute their donuts. The Red Cross has gotten on the fundraising band-wagon to be able to continue to distribute donuts Red Cross also have Donut Dollies who provide this serve too.

Researching this topic I discovered that this holiday is not the only day donuts can be enjoyed nationwide. June 8 is International Jelly-Filled Donut Day, September 14 is National Cream-filled donut Day and October 30 is Buy a Donut Day. For Donut lovers you don't have to satisfy your love for donuts only on the first Friday in June, you can enjoy them all year round.

Activities:

- Have the participants play ring toss as a representation of the donuts. If you can set up several sets of ring toss in order to accommodate all your participants.

Theme: World Juggling Day

Food:

 • Vegetables tray with carrot and celery sticks (clubs), cherry tomatoes (balls) and fruit, pineapple rings (rings) and cherries (balls) These items to resemble the juggling items. You can use other foods that could represent the juggling clubs, balls, or rings used by the jugglers.

Crafts:

 • Tennis balls filled with rice and closed with duck tape or balloons filled with sand or bird seed.

 • Print the picture of the court jester juggling and have the participants paint the pictures.

History:

If you are tossing rings, balls, clubs, knives or fire in the air and catching it, you must be a juggler. World Juggling day began in the year 1947 when individuals who love this sport decided to come together and enjoy tossing things in the air together. The idea of getting together is to help spread the enthusiasm for the sport for new jugglers and to hone the sport to perfection, for entertaining the audiences enjoying the show.

Jugglers can use many objects to toss in the air to entertain the crowd. The juggler usual tosses 3 objects such as balls, clubs, that look like bowling pins, or rings in the air and catches them. As the juggler advances, they are able to juggle 4, 5, 6 or more objects at one time. Some more advanced jugglers even juggle knives, fire torches, or running chainsaws.

These aren't the only juggling items that performance use to entertain their audiences. Some jugglers want to make their audiences laugh so they may juggle toilet plungers, rubber chickens, or miss matched objects. Some use diabolo, devil sticks, poi, spinning plates, and cigar boxes. (get pictures of these different juggling items for the participants to see) which are less popular juggling items used. Jugglers have to practice long hours to perfect their skills in order to entertain and wow their audience.

Jugglers have been around for quite some time. Court jesters used juggling moves to entertain the Royal courts. Ancient drawings also displayed pictures of jugglers on the walls within Egyptian tombs. Writings from Rome, China, and Ireland have references to jugglers in their books as well. So many places have seen the fun entertainment of a juggler. Some were not so happy to see a juggler. They thought that they were witches and often punished for their display of this "magical entertainment." James Ernest, wrote in his *Contact Juggling* book, that juggling is; "a visually complex or physically challenging feat using one or more objects, which most people do not know how to do, and which has no apparent purpose other than entertainment." In short it's the art of manipulating objects in a constant motion in the air or bouncing on the floor, hopefully without dropping the objects.

Now try your hand at juggling.

Activities:
- Get 3 scarves for each participant and have them try to juggle. Get instructions off the internet how to teach them to juggle. The scarves will fall slower than balls allowing participants to be

successful. Or get some juggling balls for the participants to try their hand at this art.

- Get a juggler to demonstrate the art of juggling and to help the participants try to juggle.

- Or get a video off the Internet to see a juggler juggle.

Theme: Superman Celebration - June 7th

Food:

* Vegetables tray with dip. Fruit tray. Drink

Crafts:

* Make superhero masks. Provide masks, paint, felt, foam and other craft items to decorate the masks.

History:

"It's a bird, it's a plane, no it's Superman," are the words that people would say when they saw the flash of light, when Superman came on the scene. This super hero has been around since 1933 and was created by writer Jerry Siegel and artist Joe Shuster. These two guys were high school students in Cleveland, Ohio when they created Superman and began the story of his life.

The story began on the planet Krypton, but Superman was the only survivor on the planet. His father, Jor-El, realized that his planet was about to blow up from a nuclear chain reaction building inside the core, and wanting to save his son, he sent him into space landing on Earth. As he landed on Earth he was born and Jonathan and Martha Kent rescued him from inside the space capsule. The Kents took the baby, named him Clark and raised him as their own in Smallville, Kansas.

The Kents were not aware of Clark's superhuman powers when his Kryptonian body began developing. When he turned eighteen they took him to the spacecraft where he was born, which was still hiding where it crashed. After learning his birth story, he left for college at Metropolis University.

Clark Kent worked privately to prevent disasters from occurring to people in his community, but a major disaster occurred that made Superman have to go public to save a NASA space-plane from crashing. To keep his identity a secret, his parents made him a costume he wore when he was fighting crime. He took on the name "Superman" which was given to him by Lois Lane, a reporter of the Metropolis Daily Planet newspaper. Clark later joined the reporting staff of The Metropolis Daily Planet paper too.

Since Superman was a native from Krypton, he possesses superhuman powers drawn from the red and yellow sun of Krypton. This superhuman strength made his body virtually indestructible. His superhuman powers included super hearing, telescopic vision, x-ray vision, and microscopic vision which allowed him to access a situation in a minutes, in order to respond instantly. Therefore he is able to save lives due to his many superhuman powers.

Although Superman has these superhuman powers, he has one substance that he must look out for – Kryptonite radiation, because it will kill him in minutes. He is also powerless to magic, and to his nemesis Braniac. Another superpower is when he fills his lungs with air when he flies. He can last for hours without replenishing the oxygen.

This Superhero has spanned a few decades for readers to enjoy. Their first 5 issues "The Reign of the Superman," are rare and were sold for $50,000 years later. Then they produced a different concept for their superhero and sold it to newspapers syndicates, but it was unsuccessful. The comic was put in a draw and later pulled out for the photo of the Superhero holding a car above his head and used for the cover of the Action

Comic magazine. The publishers asked Siegel and Shuster if they could put together a 13 page story to go with the photo. The two quickly cut and pasted their newspaper comic strips into a comic book format and sent it to Action Comic magazine. The comic was published and was a big success. This skyrocketed the sales of the Superman Comics strip issue of Action Comic magazine.

Siegel and Schuster sold their rights for $130 dollars and a contract to supply the publisher with superhero comics. This was sent to The Saturday Evening Post in 1960 who paid Siegel and Shuster $75,000 each per year. The two guys were only receiving a fraction of the profit and sued for more money. In the legal battle they accepted $200,000, but had to sign away the rights to the Superman character, and were off the byline of the comic strip. The Superman character was featured in the DC Comics

After the first comic strip was published Superman was released in theaters in 1948 and 1950 animated cartoon shorts. It wasn't until 1951 when the first movie was released titled, *"Superman and the Mole Men,"* The Superman rights was purchased by Ilya and Alexander Salkind and Pierre Spengler in 1974 and they released Superman in 1978, and Superman II in 1980. Three years later Superman III and the next year a Supergirl film. The rights were sold again to Cannon films who produced Superman IV: The Quest for Peace. Over the next fifteen years Superman Returns, followed by Superman II: The Richard Donner Cut.

Several actors that played Superman over the years. The original actor was George Reeves, followed by Christopher Reeves and in 1940's the actor was Kirk Alyn and the voice for the original cartoon of Superman was Bud Collyer.

Activities:

- Watch some Superman shorts cartoons.
- Lead a discussion on why Superman has been so popular through the years.

JULY

Theme: National Ventriloquism Week – July 16 – 19

Decoration: Search the Internet for pictures of the puppets that ventriloquists use. You can decorate with different puppets.

Food:

- Cupcakes with different faces on them. Coffee/tea, milk. You can have the cupcakes baked and have the participants decorate the cupcakes with icing and other decorations to make faces on them for the characters that the ventriloquists use to perform with.

Crafts:

- Make puppets out of white long athletic socks . Then get goggle eyes, felt, feathers, ribbons, scraps of materials and anything that might work to decorate their puppet.

History:

One might be surprised that the roots of Ventriloquism was around the 6th century and the ventriloquist used the "throwing of his voice" to supposedly communicate with the dead. It was believed at that time that the spirit of the dead went to the depths of the "prophets" stomach and lived there, and that is why the ventriloquist were able to communicate as the deceased. In the courts of King Francis the 1st was when this practice began with a well known ventriloquist of the time, Louis Brabant. Brabant used his talent in this manner to secure a job in the kings court. It was believed that these prophets could predict the future by listening to the "belly spirits" who had an insight about the future. In fact the name, ventriloquist, literally means, "belly speaker" in Latin. This hoax of the time allowed the ventriloquist to gain power and prestige in the 6th century courts.

Ventriloquism had a negative view in the Christian church, feeling that this practice was sacrilegious and an act of superstition and devils worship. But soon that notion changed when Fred Russell, in the 19th century came up with a wooden doll like figure that he performed with. This performance was quite entertaining for the audience as the character interacted with Russell. Finally, ventriloquism got its start as a form of entertaining and the crowds loved it. Russell became known as the "Father of modern ventriloquism."

Russell inspired many to follow in his footsteps. The famous Edgar Bergen with his dummy sidekick Charlie McCarthy. This act was popular in 1938 and he became and international success. He was followed by Buffalo Bob Smith who's character was the beloved Howdy Doody. Smith even performed on kids show, Howdy Doody Time, for ten years. Kids and grownups enjoyed gathering around the TV to see what adventures he would have next. Kids shows didn't end with this ventriloquist. Everyone remembers Shari Lewis with her cast of puppets in the 1940s through the 1960s with her "Shari Lewis Show." She had her most famous puppet, Lamb Chop, followed by Charlie Horse, Hush Puppy, and Wing Ding. Today the most famous ventriloquist is Jeff Dunham who's puppets include, Walter, Peanut, Jose Jalapeno on a Stick, Achmed the Dead Terrorist, Melvin the Superhero Guy, Bubba J, and Sweet Daddy Dee.

Unlike many of his predecessors, however, Dunham's show is not kid-friendly and is loaded with adult material.

This form of entertainment takes a lot of practice to convey the illusion that the dummy or puppet is talking. Ventriloquists have the difficult task of interacting with the "dummy," changing the voice from when they are talking, manipulate the controls for the mouth, eyes and other facial parts that are included in their puppet, follow the story, and oh, yes, doing this without moving their lips when the "dummy" is talking. A good ventriloquist is able to do all this which makes the "dummy" come alive to the audience. This art form is quite entertaining. So the next time you see a ventriloquist consider how versatile they are to be able to perform all these task looking like it is nothing.

Activities:

- Have a ventriloquist come to perform.
- Watch old clips of Fred Russell, Edgar Bergen, Buffalo Bob Smith, Shari Lewis or Jeff Dunham (note: Jeff Dunham's program can have inappropriate themes)
- Use these instructions on the Internet on "How to be a good Ventriloquist," and have the group try to be a ventriloquist.

Theme: National Ice Cream Birthday

Food:

- Ice Cream and all the fixings

Craft:

- Make a container or two of homemade ice cream. Allowing the clients to participate in the making.

History:

The Victorian era had a wild imagination and brought several stories of how ice cream began. The three legends are as follows: Marco Polo brought Ice Cream from China, even though he never went to China. The next story was that Catherine de' Medici introduced it to France and the third legend said that King Charles the 1st had his own personal ice cream chief.

Although Marco Polo didn't bring ice cream from China, ice cream did originate in China during the Tang period (A.D. 618 - 907). The early discovery of using ice and salt to bring the freezing temperature to -14C to freeze buffalo, cows' and goats' milk. This process was done after heating it and allowed to ferment was the early process of making ice cream. The milk mixture was then mixed with camphor for flavoring and chilled with ice and salt. Flour was used for thickening and then the mixture was put in the freezer until hard. King Tang of Shang had 94 ice-men from his 2,271 staff who made the King his ice cream desserts.

The true creator of ice cream is not known, but the thought is that it began in 1230 -1270 in China. In the 4th Century, Arabs used different salts in their process of freezing different animal's milks into ice cream. The process of making ice cream wasn't brought to Europe until 1503. One night as a party trick, a chemist used various acids, water and salts and made a sorbet. His sorbet was a hit, but this process of freezing different milks and juice didn't take off either until 1660's. Finally later that year this process spread to Naples, Florence, Paris and Spain. In 1664 ice cream was made in Naples with sweetened condensed milk.

In 1671 ice cream was introduced at a banquet at Windsor Castle, during the Feast of St. George. Although it was served, not all the guest got to taste it. King Charles the 2nd served white strawberries and ice cream to those sitting only at the Royal table. Interest grew and wealthy people built ice house on their properties for ice cream making. Many became interested in trying to freeze creams and milks to make ice cream, but it still was not perfected for sales for the general public.

Recipes for ice cream were highly guarded by the makers, but the first recipe surfaced in 1718 in England. Method of making ice cream in the 18th century were being perfected by many. The French used a custard base with egg yolks in their process, which gave the ice cream a richer taste. Finally in 1744, America got their first experience with ice cream when Maryland Governor William Bladen's guest introduced it to America. The New York Gazette advertised ice cream for the first time in May 1777.

Presidents got on the band wagon of enjoying and serving ice cream. In 1790 George Washington was known to have spent $200 on ice cream that summer. Dolly Madison ordered a strawberry ice cream creation to serve at her husband's inaugural banquet at the White

House in 1813. Ronald Reagan enjoyed ice cream so much that he declared July 15, 1984 as National Ice Cream Day, which was also signed into law.

Ice cream remained a dessert for the wealthy until the 1800's. In 1874 the birth of soda shops sprang up in the United States. The invention of ice cream sodas, made with ice cream, chocolate syrup, and carbonated water was created to enjoy. The job of "Soda Jerk" was started to teach people how to make the ice cream sodas, Sundays and other delicious ice cream treats. Religious critics began complaining about people enjoying such a sinful creation on Sundays, so the creation of "Sundays" were developed which left out the carbonated water, which satisfied the religious critics. Later the spelling of "Sunday" was changed from ending in a "y" to end with an "e." This would further separate this enjoyable treat with the Sabbath.

In 1843 making ice cream was made easier with the invention of the ice cream maker. The wooden outer container holds the ice and salt, which causes the freezing process. An inner metal cylinder holds the milk or custard mixture. Originally they were hand cranked, stirring the mixture producing the rich delicious ice cream. Now these ice cream makers are electric, saving the arms of the makers for eating the treat instead of turning the crank on the ice cream maker. This invention allows America the opportunity to enjoy ice cream whenever they like and making it with the fresh summer fruits and berries.

In the 19th century with the processing of ice, ice cream was manufactured for the general public. Norway, Canada and America all enjoyed having this tasty treat. Ice was sold to ice cream makers and shipped to major ports all over the world. Immigrants were given ice cream as a welcome, when they landed at Ellis Island New York when coming to America.

Activities:

- <u>Fun Facts Activity</u> – you can write them on strips or 3x5 cards and pass them out to the group to have them participate by reading the facts.

  ✓ On average, Americans eat 23.2 quarts of ice cream, sherbet, ices and other frozen dairy products each year.

  ✓ A single cone of ice cream takes 50 licks to finished

  ✓ What flavor is the most popular? Vanilla, Chocolate or Strawberry? (That is the order of popularity)

  ✓ In the United States ice cream must contain 10% of milk fat to label it as ice cream. The interesting thing is that it is not the major ingredient-- air is.

  ✓ When enjoying ice cream you may have experienced "brain Freeze." This is when blood vessels in the head dilate triggered when the cold ice cream touches the roof of your mouth.

  ✓ William Breyer hand cranked his first freezer of ice cream in 1866. He enjoyed making ice cream so much that he opened his first shop in 1882 cranking his cream all by hand. He also would deliver it to his customers with his horse-drawn ice wagon.

✓ Blue Bell ice cream grew out of local a group of Texas farmers. They opened the Brenham Creamery Company, located in Brenham, Texas, to make butter from their excess cream. In 1907 farmers decided to begin making ice cream to add to their product line. In 1930 their name was changed to the Blue Bell Creamery to highlight the beautiful bluebell wildflowers that grow in Texas and beautify the states landscape.

✓ The invention of Dippin' Dots, was a method of flash freeze using nitrogen. This process was invented by a graduate of Southern Illinois University, Curt Jones. This product has to be kept at minus 40 degrees Fahrenheit so it is not sold in grocery stores, but is found in places like ball games, and fairs that have the small specialize freezers for this product.

✓ In 1920, chocolate-coated ice cream bars on a stick came on the scene called a Good Humor bar. Creator Harry Burt created a way to sell ice cream on a stick allowing a quick way to serve ice cream. He purchased 12 trucks with freezer units built in that would drive through neighborhoods, ringing a bell and distribute ice cream on the street. This was a popular summertime treat for families and kids. The Good Humor men were required in the beginning to tip their hats to ladies and salute men.

✓ The Dairy Queen has an interesting beginning in 1938. They offered all you can eat soft ice cream dessert for ten cents, in Kankakee, Illinois. That day they served 1,600 people in 2 hours and the tasty treat was a hit. Out of that one day of all you can eat treats, Dairy Queen was born.

✓ Ben & Jerry ice cream was invented by two childhood friends, Ben Cohen and Jerry Greenfield. After having unsuccessful career paths they decided to look elsewhere. They thought first about selling bagels but the equipment for making them was too expensive. They discovered a $5 course on how to make ice cream, took it, and the rest is history. They opened their first successful ice cream store in a college town and called it Ben & Jerry's. Now you can find this ice cream in most grocery stores too.

✓ Baskin Robbins began in 1945 when Burton Baskin and Irvine Robbins wanted to start an ice cream parlor where people could gather to socialize while enjoying their ice cream treats. They also wanted to offer a variety of flavors and made 21 different options for their customers to choose from. This ice cream shop concept brought repeat customers and that is why Baskin Robbins 31 Flavors is so success even today. By 1948 they had open 6 full service stores.

Theme: National Hot Dog Day – July 23

Decorate the room like a fair or carnival.

Food:

- Hot dogs of course, and all the different fixings: mustard, catchup, onions, relish, sauerkraut, chili, slaw, and any other condiments that are popular where you live. You may serve chips and soft drinks to complete the snack.

Crafts:

- Have a contest of who can make the best playdough or clay hot dog in a bun.
- Or you can use construction paper for the bun and hot dog and use red and yellow string for the catsup and mustard

History:

Processing meats to preserve for the winter is a common event in many countries. Sausages were even mentioned in 9 B.C. in the story of Homer's Odyssey. So where did the hot dog come from and who should gets the credit for inventing it? It is a common belief that Germany should get the credit. The city of Frankfurt, tradition says, created the "dachshund" or "little-dog," but this fact has been disputed by Johann Georghehner, a butcher in Coburg, Germany. In 1600's Coburg traveled to Frankfurt to promote his new product. His "little dogs" sausages were a hit and spread quickly throughout Germany.

Stories of where the hot dog started are everywhere. The city of Frankfurt has said to have celebrated the hot dog's 500th birthday in 1987, five years before Christopher

Columbus came to America. Citizens of Vienna, Austria claim they were the birthplace of the hot dog. They started calling it "wiener" to go along with their claim after their city Wien where it was produced. The real story might be a mix of many nationalities. Processing meat became popular so butchers wouldn't waste any part of the meat product, grinding it into a sausage or "hot dog" became common place in several countries.

Our North America hot dog was first seen in 1860 when a German immigrant began selling hot dogs from a food cart in New York City's Bowery. This quick lunch became a hit for the workings in that area and in the Bronx, so much so, that they sold 3,684 dachshund sausages in a milk roll bun during the first year.

The hot dog grew in popularity and in 1893 Chicago got on the food cart band-wagon, selling hots dogs on the street too. Patrons were happy with the hot dog because they were quick and easy to eat and not hard on their wallets. The popularity of the easy to eat hot dog grew to many venues. Ball parks started serving them to patriots in the stands. Fair-goers also enjoyed this tasty treat as they walked around the fair grounds.

So how did the hot dog get its name? The "hot dog" legend claims that it got its name in 1901 on the New York Polo Grounds. It was a cold day at the Polo match when the vendors thought they would entice the crowd to purchase their food by announcing that the items were "hot." Tad Dorgan, a sports cartoonist from the New York Journal, noticed the vendors attempts to sell more food by saying it was hot. This caught his eye and he began to create a cartoon to go with this scenario. As he watched this scenario play out he decided to draw a barking sausage. Not sure how to spell "dachshund" he just wrote "hot dog." Despite Dorgan's popular cartoon drawings, historians could never locate this historic cartoon picture to verify this story. Whether it is true or not, it makes a good ending to our story of how the hotdog got its name.

Activities:

• Surf the Internet for the video on How Hotdogs are made. A five minute clip that is very interesting and informative makes a great introduction to a special festivity.

• Surf Internet for fun fact about hotdogs.

• Have a hotdog bar and allow seniors to fix a hotdog with their favorite fixings. Then have them share memories of times when they enjoyed a hotdog with someone special or at a special event.

Theme: National Milk Chocolate Day

Food:

> • Serve Swiss milk chocolate candy or other brands of milk chocolate like Hershey, Nestle or other. Also serve chocolate milk.

Crafts:

Pinterest has several Hershey kisses crafts that would be fun for the participants.

> • Mouse craft – To make the mouse, glue two candy kisses together bottom to bottom. Before you glue them together put two round ears on one flat side and small goggle eyes on the one of the pointy side of a chocolate kiss.

> • Rose craft - Take two red or pink foil Hershey kisses glued flat sides together, then take clear plastic wrap over the kisses and attach to a skewer with green floral tape. You can get some leaves to attach to the stem skewer, and cover entire stem with the green floral tape. This would complete the rose bud.

History:

Milk Chocolate lovers owe a big thank you to Daniel Peter for his development of milk chocolate. Peters life did not begin in the chocolate business, rather he worked as a Latin teacher at age 19, and in a grocery store for a widow Madame Clement. In the summer 1852 he also worked in her candle factory. This experience helped to build his self-esteem, due to the confidence Madame Clements had for him. His brother joined him in the candle-make factory and they improved the candles which at the time was the main light source. Four years later Peter and his brother ran the company for Madame Clements. The brothers did so well that they purchased a larger work space in Vevey, Switzerland.

During his work experience he met and married Fanny Cailler the eldest daughter of the Caillers. As kerosene was discovery in 1864, it sent the sales of candles plummeting. The Peter brothers decided to look into other avenues of revenue. Daniel Peters asked to join his brother-in-law, August Cailler chocolate business, but he was not interested in this business agreement. So Daniel decided to go into the chocolate business on his own.

Daniel was a very motivated worker continuing to make candles and working on perfecting his chocolate creations. In order to know as much as possible about the chocolate production he took a job in the chocolate factory in Lyon, France for a few weeks. He spent all his extra time studying and perfecting the mechanics and chemistry of milk chocolate. He also researched the cocoa production for the best flavors.

Daniel continued working on his formula for the best chocolate when he became friends with his neighbor, Henry Nestle. Nestle's business was making baby food, which used "milky flour" in the process. Daniel decided to incorporate chocolate in the milky flour and continued to work on perfecting it while his brother Julien worked in the candle shop. In 1869, Daniel's brother Julien died, forcing him to run both sides of their business. Finding it too difficult to run both businesses Daniel gave up the candle-making business and made and sold chocolates in the daytime and worked on a more stable product composed of cocoa, sugar and milk leaving out the milk flour that Nestle used.

Daniel's discovery was a breakthrough in the milk chocolate process, but he was unable to purchase the machinery to produce the product. Trying several processes to produce the milk powder without it spoiling were unsuccessful., but Daniel never gave up. Finally, in 1887 Daniel developed a chocolate that would not go rancid on the shelf, and it was the first successful milk chocolate product in the world. The product was named, "Gala" which means in Greek, 'from the milk." This is the delicious Swiss Chocolate that we still enjoy today.

Activities:
Make no bake Fudge:
8 ozs **cream cheese**

- 4 cups **confectioners' sugar**
- 11/2 tsps **vanilla extract**
- 12 ozs **milk, dark or white chocolate** (chopped)
- 1/4 cup **chopped pecans** (optional)

Directions

1. Grease an 8x8 inch baking dish. Set aside.
2. In a medium bowl, beat cream cheese, sugar, and vanilla until smooth.
3. In the top of a double boiler over lightly simmering water, heat milk, dark or white chocolate, stirring until melted and smooth.
4. Fold melted chocolate and pecans into cream cheese mixture. Spread into prepared baking dish. Chill for 1 hour, then cut into 1 inch squares.

AUGUST

Theme: National Root Beer Float Day

Food:

- Root beer and vanilla ice cream to make floats to enjoy. These can be served in mason jars for a fun change.

Crafts:

- Use mason jars and put painters tape onto the jar to cover sections in a design. Then go outside and spray paint the jar with silver, gold or other color of spray paint. When dry, you can peel off the tape and you will have a fun flower vase. Purchase artificial flowers to put in the jars to decorate their room.

History:

Root beer float, or "black cow," was created by Frank Wisner in the 19th century. And even today this delicious treat is enjoyed by children and adults alike. So how did Root Beer floats come about? Well one night when kids were visiting Wisner's company, the Cripple Creek Cow Mountain Gold Mining company, he gave them a drink of Meyers Avenue Red Root Beer. Wanting to make the refreshments he served more special, he added ice cream to the Root Beer. This combination was born while staring at the moon hovering over Cow Mountain. When he saw the moon this way it gave him an idea to put ice cream into the children's soda. The next day while children were visiting he added the vanilla ice cream and the root beer float was born. This ice cream treat was an immediate hit. People would continue to come to the

Cripple Creek Cow Mountain Gold Mining Company to get this enjoyable treat.

Root beer was invented by an Arizona pharmacist who mixed 16 herbs, spices, barks, and berries to make a delicious beverage. In 1919 Roy Allen purchased his recipe and produced this delicious carbonated soda for public consumption. Allen started with a small Root Beer Stand in Lodi, California for his patrons to enjoyed, and he served it in a unique way - in a frosted mug. His Root Beer stand became a popular hangout, and Allen wanted to establish more stands throughout California. Partnering with Frank Wright, who worked for him at his original stand, they opened several more stands. This is when the name, "A&W" was born. Using the first letter of their last names became the name of their Root Beer. With the new name, they began establishing A&W franchises and the first chain restaurant was established. They began serving food as well at their stands to accompany the root beer floats. Over the years their franchises grew and expanded throughout the West and Midwest.

Activities:

- Set the room up like an old fashioned soda shop. Listen to Rock & Roll music. Plaid table cloths can help set the theme. Swap stories of the most interesting places that seniors enjoyed a root beer float.

Theme: National Clown Week
August (1-7)

Find and display pictures of the famous clowns such as Bozo, Ronald McDonald, Emmett Kelly, Clarabell, and Red Skelton's Freddy the Freeloader.

Food:

- See if McDonalds will provide happy meals for each participant and have Ronald McDonald in costume bring them to the facility and share some fun.

Crafts:

- A sewing store or on line purchase a clown doll pattern for participants to make. You can hand sew them together or glue the clown dolls together with a fabric body. Use yarn for the hair and little Styrofoam balls for the head, goggle eyes or buttons for eyes.

History:

Brightly colored clothes, white or scruffy faces, fake red nose, silly hair, big shoes and gloves and you know that a clown has entered the room. Some people are fearful of clowns, but the intention of a clown is to brighten one's day, bring smiles to the sick children, and make people laugh. Because of the charitable work by clowns, President Richard Nixon in 1971 declared August 1 – August 7 as National Clown Week in honor of their work.

Let's look at where clowning began. First the word, "clown," came from a Scandinavian word, "clod," which means coarse or boorish fellow. This describes the nature of clowning having to be forward in their presentation to the crowd. In Rome and Greece you saw clowns on the stage with the burlesque shows. In the Middle Ages, kings' courts had fools, court jesters and clowns who entertained for different events. The entertainers often had many talents like playing musical instruments, juggling, mime, acrobatics and dance. These entertainers wore brightly colored costumes and performed flamboyant acts for the pleasure of the royal court.

Throughout time we have seen many famous clowns, starting with Bozo the Clown. This fun loving clown had a TV show called, "Bozo's Big Top," later changed to "Bozo's Circus." This Chicago produced show for kids began in 1949 and ran through 2001. Kids huddled around their television sets to see the funny antics Bozo had for that days show.

Another famous clown can be seen everywhere as you drive around any town , you guessed it - Ronald McDonald. This fun loving clown offers a smile to any child's face whether it is in the restaurant eating a happy meal or visiting the hospital for ill children. Families and kids of all ages enjoy this happy white faced clown, with orange hair, red and white strip socks, and yellow coveralls.

The next clown is the legendary ring leader for the famous, Ringing Brothers and Barnum & Bailey Circus. "Weary Willie" came to life during the depression era, hoping to add a smile and levity to the worries of life at the time. Later numerous movies and TV shows were produced featuring Weary Willie this legendary clown.

Another of the famous clown seen on the TV show, Howdy Doody was Clarabell the Clown . This noted clown was the infamous sidekick of Howdy Doody. This clown never talked until the very last episode when he said "Good-Bye" with a tear in his eye.

Clown troups have been used by churches to reach people in ways that others can not, by breaking down the barriers of a face to face encounter, with their colorful costumes and silly antiques. People often feel able to interact with a clown more easily because they break down walls with laughter.

Activities:
Show You Tube clips of famous Clowns such as

- Bozo the Clown
- Ronald McDonald visit
- Emmett Kelly
- Clarabell the Clown

Have a clown parade. Encourage seniors to dress up as a clown using materials and make up on hand. Give a small prize for the most inventive or creative outfits, noses, and make-up.

Theme: National Radio Day

Food:

- Popcorn and soda

Crafts:

- Purchase a small wooden box for each participant. They can decorate it to look like an old time radio or they can just paint or stain them however they would like. Look on line for small wooden boxes or go to a local craft store. The participants can use the box to put things in. Adjust the pattern to fit your box.

**(3.5" x 2.5" x 1 1/2") MAKE A PATTERN OF AN OLD FASHIONED RADIO

History:

The radio was invented in the late 1800's making receiving information easier and more entertaining. This wireless radio was due to the invention of the telegraph and the telephone. The invention of the radio allowed music, and speech to enter into every households who owned a radio. Families would gather around the radio after dinner to hear important speeches, stories, or enjoy music with the family.

Several inventors had a part in the invention of the radio. It began with Hans Christian Orsted in 1820 who made the connection between electricity and magnetism. Three other men joined in the working on the invention, Andre'-Marie Ampere, Joseph Henry, and Michael Faraday. All of these men worked on the process resulting in James Clerk Maxwell developing the theory of electromagnetism which was the process needed for radio waves. Even though Maxwell developed it, David Edward Hughes worked further on the process. But it wasn't until 1887 and 1890 when the first systematic transmission was performed by Heinrich Rudolf Hertz. In 1910, the process was first called a "radio."

Radio Day began in the 1920 in the United States and by 1928 the US and had three radio stations. Large audiences listened for entertainment and information especially throughout the Great Depression in the 30's and WWII. President Franklin D. Roosevelt used the power of the radio to address the public with his famous "fireside chats." This was a great medium for Roosevelt to disseminate pertinent information to the listeners.

Radio Day was first observed in 1945 in the Soviet Union and next it was observed in Bangladesh. National Radio Day spread across the world. The transmission of information and music in this manner was a stepping stone for the world of information.

Although the radio played an important roll in communicating information across America and around the world, National Radio Day did not come about until the 1990s.

Activities:

- Reminisce about your favorite radio show.
- Produce a radio show by assigning different parts to each participant to perform. For example: have one person do the weather, one to do the news, one the DJ, one do a special interest story, etc.
- Play clips of prominent radio programs from the 1940s, 1950s, and 1960s.
- Invite a celebrity from a local radio station to talk about broadcasting.

Theme: National Relaxation Day

Food:
- Bon bons, Chocolate-coated strawberries, small cheesecake bites and other decadent foods. Sparkling cider, mock-tails, coffee/tea.

Crafts:
- Make lavender sachet pouches with nice fabric pouches.
- Make diffusers: Using essential oils, spices, herbs, essential oil of your choice fragrant wood, or flower pedals. Spice jar, cleaned thoroughly or small baby food jars
- Bamboo skewers, cut to varied lengths. Warm water or oil
- Can use olive oil and spices to make the diffuser too.
- Fill the jar with warm water and add essential oil–I used 10 drops of sweet orange. Put the lid on and arrange the skewers through the shaker holes in the lid. Place in a kid-proof part of the room to prevent spills, and you're done.

History:
Work, meetings, kids, shopping, laundry, cooking, errands and the list of obligations go on and on for everyone. Emmette Lee Dickinson was observing that this was not a good thing so he began National Relaxation Day. Dickinson did not stop there, he developed many relaxation techniques that are still being used. We all need to take time to slow down and "smell the roses," so to speak.

Stress can cause many mental and physical health problems, so it is very important for everyone to find things that you enjoy doing, and schedule time to actually do it. If you have a stressful event occur during your day, you need to take time to relax, put your feet up, take deep breaths an restore yourself from your days' events.

One of Dickinson's relaxation method is to follow 6 easy steps to enhance your stress reduction:

- Relax your mind.
- Relax your head.
- Relax your neck and torso.
- Relax your limbs.
- Relax all fingers and toes.
- Spend alone time.

Dickinson had other relaxation methods which includes, the Perceptual Deprivation Rehabilitation Chair, where a deliberate reduction of stimuli is removed from the participant. Blindfold, hoods, and earmuffs are used to eliminate stimulation from the participant. At times other methods are included to cut off the sense of smell, touch, taste, heat and gravity. Still another 1800's inventions is his Relaxation booth, where the participant is put in total isolation. This Relaxation Booth is still sold and used today.

There are several current methods to help individuals reduce stress. The first would be to **meditate.** This process includes sitting comfortably in a chair with your feet on the floor and think positive thoughts. Recite these thoughts out loud or in your mind with thoughts like, "I am at peace." "I am enjoying the day," "I am successful," or other positive thoughts.

Another stress buster is to take 5 minutes and focus on **deep breathing.** For this process you need to sit up straight, close your eyes and put your hand on your belly to make sure you are breathing deeply. Inhale through your nose and exhale through your mouth. Not only does this reduce stress it lowers blood pressure.

The third process to relax is to forget all that has or is happening that day or week. Take 5 minutes and focus on a the beach, mountains or other experience that consumed your thoughts in a good way. Therefore be in the **present.**

A good stress reducer is to talk with a friend, preferably in person, but on the phone will do. Share what is happening in your life and find out what is going on in theirs. Family phone calls can be a stress releasing activity too. So **reaching out** to another is a way to relax.

Being aware of how tense your body is and trying to focus on relaxing the tense part of your body, helps you to relax. Focusing on this process for several minutes per tense area, will reduce the stress allowing your body to relax.

The sixth suggestion is to place a warm heat wrap around your neck and shoulders for 10 minutes. Close your eyes and try relaxing your face, neck, back and upper chest. Roll a ball over your back and neck after removing the heat wrap for further stress reduction.

Lastly remember STRESSED spelled backwards is DESSERTS. So if you are not able to relax with the other suggestions you can always enjoy some dessert.

Activities:

- Have a salon or volunteers to come in to do manicures, facials, shaving for the men, or massages for the participants, making it a Spa Day for the participants. Play serene music like beach scape or instrumental.

- Look up on the Internet, Guided Imagery Scripts, Guided Meditation to lead the group in this process.

- Lead the participants through some relaxation techniques listed above.

SEPTEMBER

Theme: Grandma Moses Day
September 7, 1860

Food:

- Since Grandma Moses was born in New York , serve NY cheesecake.

Craft:

- See if anyone has one of her paintings or surf the Internet to get a few of her paintings and make a computer copy for everyone to see. They could be put on foam board and displayed around the room or smaller copies displayed on little easels on the tables. Provide colored pencils and paper for participants to try to copy her work or create their own work of art.

History:

Anna Mary Robertson Moses, better known as Grandma Moses, was born September 7, 1860 on a farm in Greenwich, New York. She was one of 10 children born to Russel and Margaret Robertson. A "hired man," working on a farm where she was a "servant," Thomas Salmon Moses, caught her eye and they were married in 1887 when she was 27 years old. The couple continued to work on four different farms in the Staunton, Virginia area for two decades and that is where they settled. She was blessed with 10 children, but six did not survive infancy. Having rough times they decided to return to Eagle Bridge, not far from Anna's birth place. They purchased their own farm and continued to work it with the help of their 4 children. Twenty two years of successful farming, tragedy came to her with the death of

Thomas. This was a hardship for Anna leaving her and her youngest son to run the farm. In 1936, when age finally made it too difficult for Anna to continue the difficult farming life, she moved in with one of her daughters.

Anna enjoyed keeping her hands busy designing beautiful embroidery pieces, but her aging arthritic hands was making it more and more difficult for to manage sewing, so her sister, Judith Stein, encouraged her to try painting. Anna soon began to enjoy painting because it was a lot easier for her hands to manipulate a brush verses a needle and thread. She tried this craft and found it to be much easier and more enjoyable then she could imagine.

Her first painting was to be a Christmas gift for the postman, because she felt that painting would be easier than heating the kitchen to make a cake for his gift. She continued to paint and most of her paintings were given to family members as "thank you" gifts. She continued painting and made over 1600 pieces in three decades. Before her fame, when she sold her paintings she would only charge $2 - $3 depending on the size of the piece. After her fame, her paintings now go for thousands of dollars depending on the size of the painting.

As her fame grew her paintings were seen in Gimbels, Museum of Modern Art and Otto Kallir's Gallery in New York City. Her paintings were also exhibited in Whyte Gallery in Washington, D.C.. Her primitive, rural, family life paintings were becoming popular in Europe and Japan as well. Her exhibits would draw the largest crowds of any artist of her time. As her popularity grew, you would see her paintings on Christmas cards, tiles and fabrics in America and abroad.

On her 100th birthday in 1960, Grandma Moses was honored for her achievements and her influence on young girls to become artists. A special day was initiated by New York Governor Nelson Rockefeller, "Grandma Moses Day," for such an influential and remarkable women. Although her fame was due to her paintings, her most prideful accomplishments were her four children, eleven grandchildren, and four great-grandchildren and her preserves.

Activities:

- Look in a mirror to try to draw yourself.
- Get paint by numbers kits and have participants paint them. Display the artwork for all to enjoy.

Theme: National Pickle Week
September 28 – October 14

Food:

   • Gather different types of pickles to taste and water to cleanse you pallet.

Crafts:

   • Line up the difference types of pickles in a row and have the residents go down and vote on which one they think is the best. Provide water in between the tastings.

History:

Where do pickles come from you might ask? Pickles have been around since 2030 BC. The delightful tasty treat began when northern Indian people brought cucumber seeds to the Tigris valley.

Pickles were even part of peoples diets all the way back to the Bible days. Numbers 11:5 and Isaiah 1:8 both mention the cucumber fields that were grown to make pickles. The consumption of pickles was one of the foods missed by the crowds while they were wandering in the wilderness for 40 years.

Napoleon and Aristotle praised the healing effects of pickled cucumbers. Who would have thought that a pickle would be such a popular commodity. Current research shows that pickles contain the good bacteria that your body needs in your intestines to stay healthy. Pickles also have a high concentration of vitamin C, helps absorb iron and has been known to help in weight loss.

The preservation of foods was an important process for travelers. Pickling cucumbers in vinegar, oil, and brine allowed travelers to carry them on long journeys without spoiling. The Romans also used this process of pickling, but sometimes added honey to mix for a little different flavor.

George Washington was a pickle lover too. He was known to have collected 476 different types of pickles in his travels. Thomas Jefferson also liked a good pickle. He said that there is nothing more enjoyable on a hot summer day. Other known connoisseurs of pickles were Emperors Julius Caesar and Tiberius, King John and Queen Elizabeth I of England, Samuel Pepys, Amerigo Vespucci and Napoleon Bonaparte. They are not the only people who enjoy a good crunch of the pickle. Adults and kids alike across America are known to dig into a pickle jar for a pickled treat.

The word "pickle" was derived in the 1400's from a Middle English word "pikel" which was a process used on meat to spicy them up. A difference derivative comes from the Dutch influence of "pekel" which is what they call a spicy brine mixture used for preserving and flavoring foods.

The Jewish culture are known to have used pickles to supplement or bulk up their diets dating back to the ancient world. Both the elite Jews and the impoverished groups from Egypt to Mesopotamia enjoyed a wide variety of pickled cucumbers.

More recently cultures are using the same process on cabbage making sauerkraut, slaw and other pickled treats. New York and other cities are known to have pickle carts vendors on the street for people to get a quick treat. Most deli's or sandwiches shops adds a pickle garnish to the plate before serving the meal.

Activities:

• Look on the Internet for fun facts about pickles to share. Contact Vlassic or other pickle producers to get promotional materials to use.

PICKLE FACTS:

• Americans consume 26-billion pickles a year. That's about nine pounds of pickles per person.

• *More than half the cucumbers grown in the U.S. are made into pickles.

• *Amerigo Vespucci, for whom America is named, was a pickle merchant before becoming an explorer.

• *Pickling has been used to preserve food for almost 5,000 years.

• *The pickle is both a fruit and a vegetable

• Create a pickle tasting event where participants can taste-test a wide variety of pickels and give their impressions of each.

Theme: International Square Dancing Month

Decorate with red gingham table clothes and Western items like cowboy hats, boots, and bandanas.

Food:

- Hot dog wrapped in crescent rolls, (pigs in the blanket). Dipping sauces. Could have baked beans or potato chips to go with the hotdog wraps.

Crafts:

- Using bandanas in several colors, cut them in 1-inch strips, or use a color pattern like red, white, blue. Take a Styrofoam wreath form and tie the bandana strips on the wreath form all the way around covering the form. This can be a decorated wreath for the participants doors.

- Or take a bandana and open it all the way. Take scissors and cut every ½ inch apart, all around the entire edges of the bandana. Make sure the cuts are about 1 inch long. Then take beads and thread them onto each piece that you just cut, and tie a knot on the edge to hold the bead on. When you decorate all the way around fold the bandana diagonally and tie the two folded ends around your neck in a ascot looking collar.

History:

If you are hearing a caller say, "swing your partner round and round," "do-si-do," and "promenade" you are enjoying square dancing. This fun form of dancing came to the United States in 1945 from England, Irish and Scotland. Square dancing is a systematic form of dance where the group of couples, listen to a person, called the "caller," tell you what direction to go in and what dance move you should be doing with your partner or others in the group. Square dancing began moving in a square shape, but additional dances have been added that are arranged in a circle, or a line.

Square dancing is a fun way to enjoy the company of others, as well as, a great way to exercise. This style of dance can be enjoyed by people of all ages. Many who square dance wear special clothing. Gentlemen wear cowboy boots, jeans, western shirts and a bolo style ties. Ladies wear full skirt dresses with hoops, cowboy boots, or jeans and a western shirt. Sometimes the couple wear matching outfits for square dancing. Another thing you might see is turquoise jewelry or leather trimming on the clothing.

The first documented square dancing was in England in the 17th century. It was also found in France and Europe. Settlers who came from these areas brought this lively form of dance to the United States when they settled here. Square dancing is also called barn dance or folk dancing, and is taught to adults and sometimes to children in school. Because of the enjoyment individuals receive square dancing, nineteen states in America have square dancing as their official state dance.

There are many different types of square dances across the world. These dances include Morris dance, English Country Dance, Caledonians and quadrille (New England style) square dance. In the United State the most popular country-style dancing is the Country-line dancing. This style has become popular at wedding and parties, allowing those who are single at the party the opportunity to dance and have fun too.

Activities:

- Have someone come in and call line dances for the participants, or have a staff who knows how to do the line dances teach them to the group.

- Have a square dance group come in to entertain the group.

Theme: Johnny Appleseed
John Chapman's Birthday - September 26, 1774

Food:

- Apple Crisp, apple cider, or apple slices.
- Or take an apple and cut up in cubes, put the cubes on toothpicks and dip in caramel. You can dip in nuts or sprinkles too.
- Or have the clients prepare apple pie bites. To make these you slice apples in wedges, roll out the store-bought crescent rolls, place apple at the pointed end, sprinkle with cinnamon and sugar and roll the dough around the apple to the large end of the dough triangle. Bake at 350 degrees for 11 -15 minutes.

Apple Crafts:

- Cut an apple in half and use as a form to decorate fabric. Dip the apple in paint and then press on paper or cloth to make a picture, frame it, or make a place mat. To do this craft you can purchase cheap place-mats from the dollar store to print on. You could use felt to make place mats too. Apples could be cut in half in both directions to create two different designs.

History: The Story of Johnny Appleseed:

In 1800s an American folk hero and pioneer in the apple farming industry, birthed the legend Johnny Appleseed. His real name was John Chapman. Born in Leominster, Massachusetts in 1774, he had a dream to grown enough apples so that no one would go hungry. This "dreamer" as he was called, wandered the country side of Ohio planting apple seeds throughout the land. Although he was known as the "dreamer" he was a researcher, organized businessman who bought and sold land, developed it into beautiful apple orchards for harvesting apples. His journey lasted for nearly fifty years producing thousands of productive apple trees throughout the Midwest.

John was eighteen years old when he and his half brother Nathaniel, who was eleven at the time, headed west planting apple trees as they went. John and Nathaniel stayed ahead of the immigrants who were settling at that time and continued moving west as they finished each orchard. Nathaniel decided to settle down with his father to farm one of the orchards, but John continued to travel westward planting apple orchards as he moved westward through the Ohio Valley Country and onto Indiana.

Although he was called the "dreamer" he was very ingenious collecting seeds from cider mills and creating nurseries along the way by fencing in saplings with fallen branches for protection, and returning to check on them periodically. He chose great locations, along streams, open fields and along roadways to plant his saplings allowing them the best opportunity for growth. As John wandered the Ohio Valley region he was endearingly called the "apple seed man" which later became Johnny Appleseed.

As John traveled along his way he never met a stranger. The adults and children looked forward to his visits because he brought news from other areas and preached from the Bible, his favorite book. The many friends he developed over the years always welcomed him back into their homes. He befriended Indian tribes learning their language enough to converse with them. He was what we call a vegetarian, living off the land and never killing animals for food. To look at him you would think he was a pauper, but quite the opposite. John accumulated more than he needed by selling his apple trees and tracts of land for cash. Although a wealthy man, he never relied on banks. He preferred to bury his money and enjoyed bartering and trading for food and clothes rather than building a bank of money for his trees. He was more interested in getting the apple trees planted across the valley then getting paid for the trees.

What did Johnny Appleseed look like you ask? Legend says that he was medium height, light brown hair and blue eyes, slender and full of energy. You may say that he was "funny looking" because of the way he dressed. He bartered with settlers for their old clothes and if he received nice looking clothes he often gave them to someone who he felt needed them more than he did. He also used coffee sacks as make-shift clothes by cutting out arms and head opening and wore them that way. He never wore shoes, not even in the winter, an his feet were so tough that rattlesnakes bite or ice and snow would not faze him. Another legend that added to his funny look was the mush pot hat he wore on his head. We think this is a wives tale because these pots were much too heavy to balance on one's head. He probably wore a castoff hat he found or made a hat from cardboard. He preferred sleeping under the stars next to a camp fire, and never built his own home to live in.

After spending fifty years planting, cultivating and selling trees, he made his last trip back to the Ohio Valley in 1842. He returned to live with his father and Nathaniel in the Ohio Valley. In March 1845 he was visiting his friend William Worth, in Indiana when he got pneumonia and died March 18, 1845 at the age of seventy-one. This was the only time that he was sick throughout his life. He is buried in an unmarked grave near Fort Wayne, Indiana.

Activities:

• Surf the Internet for Johnny Appleseed crossword puzzles and trivia to enhance your program.

• Do your participants know their apple varieties? Do a blind taste-test with slices of common types of apples and see if they can guess the variety.

• Invite the librarian to read a story about Johnny Appleseed or have a storyteller tell a story about apples.

OCTOBER

Theme: Charlie Brown and Snoopy Birthday – October 2

Decorate as the Great Pumpkin patch

Food:

- Pumpkin pie, pumpkin cookies or pumpkin bread, and apple cider to drink.

Craft:

- Carve pumpkins, or decorate pumpkins with markers, paper or foam pieces.

History:

Charles Schulz, the creator of our beloved Charlie Brown and Snoopy, appeared in the comic strip for the first time in October, 1950. Charlie Brown actually appeared three years earlier in *L'il Folks* for the St. Paul *Pioneer Press*. This column was never successful, but 3 years later Schultz' *Peanut* comic strip took off and is now the most recognizable cartoon strip in America.

Charlie Brown, the main character in the *Peanut* strip, was cast as a down trodden, unsuccessful, person who everyone made fun of. He was teased unmercifully by all his "friends," and even his dog Snoopy and the bird character Woodstock. You would label him as being bullied if it was in today's time. But despite his bad luck and constant torment by others, he always has a positive outlook on life.

The *Peanuts* gang not only was seen on the printed page, but made their TV debut in 1965 in the cartoon show, *A Charlie Brown Christmas,* and *A Charlie Brown Thanksgiving.* Both shows won Emmy awards for being such successful TV shows. Kids and adults alike gathered around the TV to see these comic strip characters come to life. Holiday theme shows were popular with Schulz, producing his third cartoon show, *It the Great Pumpkin Charlie Brown, in 1966.* Schultz didn't stop with TV, you can see his bigger than life Charlie Brown Character and his dog Snoopy on stage, in an off Broadway production, *You're a Good Man, Charlie Brown.*

In the 1980's and 1990's Charles Schultz had become a millionaire and donated millions of dollars to charity. He even was featured in *Forbes magazine* for being the most successful cartoonist of all times. In 1984, he was entered into the *Guinness World Records* for having been published in over 2,000 newspapers, and for being read by 355 million people.

Schultz' health began to decline in the 1990's, and he suffered a stroke, visual loss, memory problems and decline in interest to draw cartoons. So in December 1990, Schultz decided to retire. His last *Peanut* column was published January 3, 2000. February 12, 2000, was a sad day when a great artist and cartoonist lost his fight to cancer and died of colon cancer. Although he is gone, kid of all ages still enjoy his Peanut characters, cartoons strips, TV shows, and off Broadway shows to this day.

Activities:

- Word Search puzzle with the Peanut characters
- Show a video of pumpkin-chunkin competitions where people compete to see how far they can launch a pumpkin.

Theme: Pizza Month

Decorate like an Italian Restaurant

Food:

- All types of Pizzas.

Craft:

- Personal pan pizza for participants to make themselves. Use English Muffins and provide all the pizza fixings.

History:

There are many theories where the first pizza was developed, but the word "pizza" was documented in Italy, in the city of Gaeta, in 997 AD. Prior to the pizza, the Romans had a flat bread called Focaccia, to which they added toppings to and baked which was their first "pizza." Ancient historians has shown people adding toppings to breads as far back as the Neolithic age. Over 7,000 years ago French and Italian archaeologists discovered brick ovens where breads were baked. Historians feel that these ovens were used to make the early renditions of pizza. Greeks had the same process, topping the flat breads with herbs, onion and garlic. In 500 B.C. discoveries of where Persian soldiers used their shields to bake flat breads that they added cheese and dates, to make their "pizzas" on the battlefields. Some argue that this should not be called "pizza," because it was cooked in the battlefield instead of an oven.

Pizza ovens popped up all over Italy and in Rome. So many areas began making pizzas, and this delicious meal spread to Greece and then to America. Christopher

Columbus came to Genoa, Italy bringing tomatoes that were included in making of pizzas. Sauce was made from the tomatoes and added on top of the bread before the other toppings and then baked in the oven. When Francisco Pizzaro of Spain reached Europe, the use of tomatoes was an interesting addition on pizzas because many thought tomatoes were poisonous and to add them to pizza was a risky process. Soon this belief disappeared and everyone began adding tomato sauce to the pies. The pizza pie as Americans know it, grew out of this bold move of adding tomato sauce to the pizzas along with other ingredients.

The 16th and 17th Centuries pizza consumption grew tremendously through local peasants as well as travelers who were passing through Europe. Pizza was considered an exotic dish known as a pizzaioli.

The first pizza restaurant who baked pizzas to serve to their customers was Antica Pizzeria Port'Alba, located in Naples. Originally pizza was enjoyed by the poor patrons, but in the middle 18th century pizza meals grew as a meal for everyone when the Queen of Naples was such a big fan that she built her own brick oven to make her own pizzas.

Italy and America enjoyed pizza in 1889, when the "modern" pizza was developed. King and Queen Umberto the first, and Margherita di Savoia from Italy, were so taken by the delicious pie from Pizzeria Brandi, made by Esposito, they couldn't get enough of them. From this experience Esposito began to make a variety of pizza pies using marinara sauce with anchovies, white pizza with provolone, or creamy cheeses and basil. Sometimes he would make pizza with red, green and white items on top to resemble the Italian flag.

Today pizza is enjoyed all over the world, it may have difference sauces or toppings but the customers enjoy their pizza meal made to order.

Activities:

Pizza Toppings Find-a-Word

Pizza Toppings

```
P  S  E  U  L  M  W  V  P  K  B  J  T  B  E  H  A  K  X
L  I  R  G  J  R  S  K  Q  W  P  O  P  Z  L  R  N  G  O
H  C  N  E  A  S  D  P  D  A  B  B  K  F  T  K  C  N  Q
C  M  J  E  P  S  G  Y  R  Y  G  V  N  I  K  I  H  S  C
K  R  W  A  A  P  U  M  S  T  V  B  C  B  G  U  O  W  V
Y  G  I  C  E  P  E  A  N  U  E  H  C  V  Y  W  V  S  U
K  I  Q  X  A  S  P  P  S  Z  O  M  G  Q  H  S  I  N  G
A  K  E  I  I  W  V  L  T  K  J  L  N  G  M  H  E  O  Q
O  M  P  A  S  K  X  R  E  O  U  P  M  O  U  B  S  I  F
K  U  N  Z  V  Q  B  H  N  K  H  Y  O  I  Q  S  L  N  B
M  S  R  E  P  P  E  P  N  E  E  R  G  N  O  V  H  O  H
E  F  W  I  V  A  I  J  L  W  H  D  N  O  S  I  H  V  V
B  Y  H  E  R  D  X  I  U  S  H  P  Y  R  Y  W  W  G  R
V  R  D  T  S  D  X  E  U  O  G  E  Z  E  W  X  B  C  D
K  W  S  E  O  T  A  M  O  T  S  D  Z  P  I  H  U  O  M
W  G  H  A  M  B  U  R  G  E  R  U  W  P  O  Z  A  T  D
S  U  L  R  O  H  E  E  E  F  C  R  Y  E  D  Y  T  M  G
O  L  I  V  E  S  T  H  O  X  E  I  C  P  K  I  F  U  P
F  C  O  L  U  S  C  G  C  V  R  Z  D  H  U  P  T  E  E
```

ANCHOVIES	ARTICHOKE HEARTS	CHEESE
GREEN PEPPERS	HAM	HAMBURGER
HOT PEPPERS	MUSHROOMS	OLIVES
ONIONS	PARMESIAN	PEPPERONI
PINEAPPLE	SAUSAGE	TOMATOES

Theme: Mayberry Day

Food:

- Aunt Bee's apple, blackberry, or boysenberry pies, coffee and tea.

Craft:

- Have the participants dress like their favorite Andy Griffith Show characters. The winner could get a copied framed photo that matches the character they dressed like. Or you could have 1st, 2nd, 3rd prize ribbons for the winners.

History:

Mayberry, the setting for the beloved TV show, *Any Griffith,* is modeled after Andy Griffith's home town of Mount Airy, North Carolina. This sleepy little town is the quintessential small town that was formerly a stagecoach stop along the Ararat River. This picturesque town is beautiful located between the Blue Ridge Mountain and the Sauratown Mountains. The 1960s Andy Griffith's sitcom and the town of Mayberry, was modeled after 35 people, places and things that occurred in this sleepy little town of Mount Airy. Even the neighboring town, Mt Pilot, in the series is modeled after Mount Airy's neighboring town, Pilot Mountain.

Stars and places on the TV show are all around Mount Airy. You can stop in an have your hair cut at Floyd's Barbershop, or get your car serviced at Wally's Service Station. While your strolling around town and getting hungry, you can stop at the Snappy Diner for a pork chop sandwiches. The museum in Mount Airy has great photo opportunities with scenes of the show like the courthouse, in the jail, or sitting behind Andy's desk. And the icing on the cake is a ride in the police car that Andy and Barney drove around town and used to catch the occasional bad guys.

Andy, the star of the *Andy Griffith Show*, was born in Mount Airy, North Carolina. You are able to drive by and see the house where he was born and raised in this little town he called home. Andy isn't the only member of this beloved sitcom. The delightful but goofy side kick, Barney Fife, played by Don Knotts, always livened up the scene with his wild ideas and schemes. His hilarious antics created a dichotomy to Andy's level headed way of life, which makes for an entertaining interaction between the two. Other characters are the beloved Aunt Bee, played by Frances Bavier, and Andy's son, Opie, played by Ron Howard. Aunt Bee was the character that took care of Andy and Opie by cooking, cleaning and caring for them with her loving heart. Opie was a cute little boy that added to the life of Andy and Mayberry with his curiosity about life. Andy would always be available for life lessons about people, school and interaction with other.

Although the sitcom was popular in the 60's, you can see people catching a rerun any day of the week around nursing homes, retirement communities and private residents. These heart-warming episodes are great teaching tools for parents and grandparents alike as you view them with your kids and grand-kids.

Activities:

- Look on the Internet for people quiz or trivia about the Andy Griffith Show.
- Watch episodes of the Andy Griffith Show. Lead a discussion about what made the show such

a success. Why is it still popular in reruns all these years later?

• Hold a contest for the best impressions of Mayberry characters. Can you do Aunt Bee, Goober, Floyd the Barber, Andy, Barney Fife, Ottis, others?

Theme: National Pie Day
October 28

Food:

- A variety of pies

Craft:

- Make small pies from biscuit by pressing the dough out flat into small circles. Get different types of canned pie filling to put a spoonful of pie filling in the center of half of the rolled out biscuit dough. Then fold the circle of dough in half making a crescent shape. Then bake them in an available oven or a toaster oven for 12 -15 minutes.

History:

What does rye-crusted goat cheese and honey have to do with pies? That was what the first published pie recipe ingredients were. The actual first pie that was made was made in ancient Egypt. The pie recipes were passed on by people to the Greeks. The Romans learned about the process of making pies and were instrumental in spreading the recipe across Europe. In the 14th century the word "pie" showed up in the Oxford English Dictionary, and became a common item seen on tables across Europe. Some pies were put into pans lined with reeds instead of dough, not for eating, but for the sole purpose to hold the pie filling.

The word "pyes" came from the 12th century in England. "Pyes" had very thick crusts and very little filling. Pies were mostly filled with meat and gravy mixture early on, and was served as the meal not as dessert as we know it today. The crust of the pie was then called "coffyn" because it was baked in a loaf pan that resembles a coffin box. Another reason it was called a "coffyn" was because they baked whole fowl in the pan allowing their feet to hang out of the side.

In the 1500s Queen Elizabeth the first, had the idea of putting fruit inside the pie crusts, thus introducing the first fruit filled pies. The first delicious fruit pie she served was cherry and it was a hit. From this discovery, the English brought fruit pies to America. The early settlers continued to bake pies in loaf shaped pans, calling them "coffins," and still not eating the "coffin" shell. Later the term "coffin" was changed to "crust" as we referred to it as today.

Over the years Americans have adopted fruit pies as a tasty way to end a meal. This delicious dessert is consumed crust and all, and is filled with a variety of delicious fruit fillings. We also are known to fill the pie shells with meat and vegetables, which is known as a "pot pie," and is enjoyed as the meal for families on the go. Americans enjoy eating pies so much that we have adopted a familiar phrase over the years, "it's as American as apple pie." I guess we can thank the Egyptians for sharing that first pie recipe with the world.

Activities:

- See who can list the most varieties of pies in five minutes.
  - Discussion Questions:
    - ✓ Ask what is your favorite kind of pie?
    - ✓ Have you ever made a pie?
    - ✓ Do you remember your mom or grandmother making a pie?
    - ✓ How often did you have pie growing up?

NOVEMBER

Theme: Mickey Mouse's Birthday

Food:

> • Cheese and crackers (for a mouse meal) and soft drinks or cheesecake with coffee/tea.

Craft:

> • Have everyone try to draw Mickey Mouse. Search the Internet for instructions on how to draw Mickey Mouse.

History:

Who was born in 1928 and still looks as good as the day he was born? – Mickey Mouse. He is a little shorter and rounder, but that happens to all of us as we age, right? His clothes never fade or go out of style. Although this mouse is recognized all over the world, this iconic mouse was not the first successful character that the Disney Brothers Studio drew. In 1927, the star character was Oswald the Lucky Rabbit who had a round body, white face, big button nose, and floppy black ears. With the Rabbit gaining popularity, Disney's career ended quickly when the studio kept the rights to Oswald and hired away all the cartoonists. They offered to keep Disney for a lower salary but he refused and went out on his own. With Oswald gone, his one faithful animator, Ub Iwerks, and Disney started brainstorming about a new character. After many sleepless nights they finally came up with a character with shortened ears, a chubbier belly, and round circular ears and viola a star was born. Disney and Iwerks created short cartoons featuring this new mouse character named Mortimer. This name didn't catch on and rumor has it that Disney's wife suggested to call him Mickey – the rest is history.

The first two cartoon shorts that featured Mickey Mouse were unsuccessful, but the third titled, *Steamboat Willie*, was a hit. The success of this cartoon was due to the use of music and sound effects with the animated film. This mouse character Mickey, was a success only one year after Oswald the rabbit was sold out from under him. Disney went on to produce many cartoon shorts. After the series of shorts, Walt Disney began a marketing campaign introducing merchandise for fans to purchase and enjoy. This marketing items helped to expand Disney's popularity as people wore the shirts, hats and ears around the world.

The popularity of Mickey Mouse grew and in 1935 a Children's TV show, *The Mickey Mouse Club*, came on the scene. A young animator, Fred Moore, updated Mickey Mouse again to what we are familiar with today. Moore changed his circular body parts into more oval shaped body which allowed the character to move more freely in the cartoons series. Other changes he made were giving Mickey pupils, allowing his expressions to be more animated. He also added the signature white gloves and a shorter nose. Mickey was a happier, cuter, more appealing version attracting more young and old fans. Moore later added color to this cute character, which drew more attention to the character.

Mickey showed up in 12 more cartoons series that year, being portrayed as a football hero, a hunter, a tailor, and a symphony conductor in *Fantasia's Sorcerer's Apprentice*. His high pitched voice made people smile as he interacted with his girlfriend Minnie, his dog Pluto, and friend Donald Duck.

In the 1950s, Disney branched out into theme parks and opened his first Disney theme park in Anaheim, California, offering rides, shows and life size characters of all the Disney family that walk around the park for photo opportunities with the fans. In 1971 another theme park opened in Orlando, Florida. Disney Theme Parks continued to pop up around the world. In 1992 one opened in Marnela Vallee, France, Euro Disneyland Paris in 1994, and in Hong Kong in 1999. Mickey Mouse has become quite a celebrity and known by everyone worldwide.

Activities:

- Watch the first cartoon of Mickey Mouse – *Steamboat Willy* and also some newer Mickey Mouse Cartoons. You can find this cartoon on the Internet.

- You can also have the group sing the Mickey Mouse club song.
    - ✓ Who's the leader of the club that's made for you and me?
    - ✓ M-I-C, K-E-Y, M-O-U-S-E!
    - ✓ Hey there, hi there, ho there, you're as welcome as can be.
    - ✓ M-I-C, K-E-Y, M-O-U-S-E!
    - ✓ Mickey Mouse! (Donald Duck!) Mickey Mouse! (Donald Duck!)
    - ✓ Forever let us hold his banner high, high, HIGH, HIGH!!
    - ✓ Come along and sing the song and join the jamboree.
    - ✓ M-I-C, K-E-Y, M-O-U-S-E!

(cut short here starting in 1978)

✓ He's our favorite Mouseketeer, we know you will agree.

✓ M-I-C, K-E-Y, M-O-U-S-E!

✓ Take some fun and mix in love, our happy recipe.

✓ M-I-C, K-E-Y, M-O-U-S-E!

✓ M-I-C, K-E-Y, M-O-U-S-E!

(If you need to hear the tune you can find that on the Internet too!)

Theme: Gingerbread House

Food:

- Gingerbread cookies, maybe sugar cookies too & spiced cider, spiced tea

Craft:

- Decorate Gingerbread Houses for each participant. You can use graham crackers to make small houses for each participant. It is better if you put the houses together ahead of time so that they will be able to decorate them right away. To put the houses together you will need this icing, listed below. You will need a variety of candy to use to decorate the houses. Icing is for putting the houses together and to "glue" the candy onto the houses.

<u>Prepare icing</u> by using the 1 pound confectioners' sugar or more as needed

- 1/2 cup egg whites (3 large egg whites)
- 1/2 teaspoon cream of tartar

Mixing instructions:

Place all ingredients in a large mixing bowl and combine. Scrape down sides as you mix to insure all ingredients get incorporated into the icing. Turn the mixer to high and beat until thick and very stiff. Mixture will hold a peak when you pull the beaters from the mixture. If it holds the peaks, it is ready to construct the houses and to put on the candy decorations. Mixing should take at least 7-10 minutes.

History:

Decorating gingerbread houses and gingerbread cookies has been a family tradition in many homes and has become a family tradition marking the beginning of the holiday season. Families who have this tradition are not aware that creating gingerbread houses began in the 10th century. Even though the English were credited for introducing the gingerbread house and gingerbread men cookies, it actually began from an Armenian Monk located in Europe.

Swedish Nuns also enjoyed baking and sharing gingerbread items during the holiday. In fact they were the first group to bake and sell these gingerbread treats to raise money for the poor. Gingerbread was also found in the 16th century in the farmers markets and pharmacies. Ginger products were used by pharmacists to help with inflammation in the body, and to helps with swelling, arthritis, diverticulitis, gallbladder inflammation, and heart disease. Ginger has some healing effects on the stomach and helps restore your irritated stomach.

It was not until gingerbread made its way to Britain that we see it get painted with icing and decorated for the holidays. During this time is when the gingerbread cookie and house gained its popularity. Store windows displayed these beautifully decorated treats which built the excitement for the holidays. But it wasn't until the, *Hansel and Gretel* story for children, written by the Grimm Brothers, did the gingerbread house take off in popularity. Gingerbread houses were not only popular in Germany, but it gained popularity in America as well. Today you will see families engaged in this family traditions by building and decorating these tasty houses and cookies.

Wilton's cake decorating company has been making gingerbread house kits for several decades. This is an easy way to make sure this wonderful tradition continues during the busy holiday season by purchasing a kit to assemble when time allows.

Activities:

- Write a poem using the acrostic G- I -N-G-E-R-B-R-E-A-D- H-O-U-S-E

- Invite an area chef to speak to your group about gingerbread house construction.

- Put several large gingerbread houses together in groups and display them for the holidays. You could have people vote on their favorite gingerbread house.

- Invite area children to assist your group in building gingerbread houses. Perhaps make some to eat as well as display.

Theme: Sadie Hawkins Day

Food:
- Bow tie pasta salad, meatballs. Punch made with ginger-ale and sherbert.

Crafts:
- Copy these patterns for two different patterns to fill with hugs and kisses. Then these could be given to someone who is a friend, or needs to smile

History:

We all are familiar that Sadie Hawkins Day is when girls invite a guy they are interested in to a dance or on a date. But we might not be familiar with how this event became popular. Believe it or not, this tradition came from a comic strip created and illustrated by Al Capp, a great cartoonist.

In 1937 Capp created a comic strip featuring a group of poor mountain hillbillies of Dogpatch, Kentucky. In his comic strip the women were not the most attractive women in the world, in fact they were kind of homely, well all the women in town, except Daisy Mae Scraggs. These women, except Daisy Mae, had no hope in catching the most sought after bachelor, Li'l Abner, Abner's goal in life was to dodge the marriage bullet at all costs, even though Daisy Mae was a voluptuous and sexy creature that any man would love to marry. Daisy Mae always has great plans of how to catch Abner which always seems to fail. This cat and mouse game with Daisy Mae and Abner lasted in the comic strips for 18 years, pulling the readers into the Scragg's family goal for Daisy Mae - to marry Abner.

In Capp's 1937 comic, Li'l Abner, he created a day called Sadie Hawkins Day. This day was actually named after one of the homely ladies in town, giving her a chance to catch a husband. All the ladies in town were allowed to "chase" in whatever way they could, to capture the man and marry them by the end of that day. This reverse attack caused the men in town, especially the highly sought after, Li'l Abner, to spend the day running away from the women in town.

Finally, March 31, 1952, Daisy Mae Scragg was able to catch and marry Li'l Abner which became a major event, even making the cover of *Life Magazine.* The article, *It's Hideously True!! The Creator of Li'l Abner Tells Why His Hero Is Wed!!,* also illustrated by Capp for the magazine.

After building the interest of girls chasing boys that didn't want to be caught, *Sadie Hawkins Day* was created in 1937. Schools began to hold "Sadie Hawkins" Dances which allowed girls the opportunity to invite the boy who they may have a crush on to the dance, without it being awkward. Sometimes it became a good way for shy boys to get a date with the girl he wanted to ask out too. These dances began in November but now happen anytime from November to February.

Leap year is another day that has become part of the "Sadie Hawkins" theme. For women who have been dating a man for awhile and feel that marriage is the next step, may ask their boyfriend to marry them on the 29th day of February – Leap year. This allows women to take the next step when their guys might have cold feet about getting married. Unfortunately for those relationships, this day only happens once every four years.

So depending on what side of the fence you are on, you can look forward to Sadie Hawkins Day – or Not!

Activities:

- Name match famous couples

- Show the movie, Li'l Abner (1hr 15 min DVD up to 2 hour DVD depending on the movie you select)

- Print off some Li'l Abner comic strips to have on the tables for participants to read.

- For the really ambitious, hold a Sadie Hawkins dance and allow the ladies in the group to ask the men to dance.

Famous Couples
(fill in the blanks)

1, Romeo	_____	Juliet
2. Lucy Ball	_____	Desi Arnaz
3. Fred Flintstones	_____	Wilma Flintstones
4. Ethel Mertz	_____	Fred Mertz
5. Barney Rubble	_____	Betty Rubble
6. Cleopatra	_____	Mark Antony
7. George Burns	_____	Alicie Allen
8. Richard Burton	_____	Elizabeth Taylor
9. Scarlet O'Hara	_____	Rhett Butler
10. Adam	_____	Eve
11. Odysseus	_____	Penelope
12. Brad Pitt	_____	Angelina Jolie
13. Bonnie Parker	_____	Clyde Barrow
14, Demi Moore	_____	Ashton Kutcher
15. Elvis Presley	_____	Priscilla Presley
16. Franklin Roosevelt	_____	Eleanor Roosevelt
17.George W. Bush	_____	Laura Bush
18. George Washington	_____	Martha Washington
19. Goldie Hawn	_____	Kurt Russell
20. Ike Eisenhower	_____	Mamie Eisenhower
21. Jennifer Garner	_____	Ben Affleck
22. Jennifer Lopez	_____	Marc Anthony
23. John F. Kennedy	_____	Jackie Kennedy
24. John Lennon	_____	Yoko Lennon
25. John Travolta	_____	Kelly Preston
26. Roy Rogers	_____	Dale Evans
27. Ronald Reagan	_____	Nancy Reagan
28. Sonny	_____	Cher

Theme: Charles Dickens

Food:
- Rice pudding, spiced tea

Crafts:
- Take an orange and poke holes in it and fill the hole with whole cloves. Use a toothpick or shesh-kabob skewer to poke the holes. This project makes a wonderful Christmas potpourri for the holidays.
- Or take the cinnamon-scented pine cones and tie red ribbon around the top of three pine cones and tie the three ribbons together with a bow at the top to hang them on your door for a wonderful smelling holiday decoration.

History:

Famous British novelist, Charles Dickens, was born in 1812, in Portsmouth, England to John and Elizabeth Dickens. He was one of eight children who enjoyed exploring Rochester Castle and running free in the countryside. Charles' dad worked as a naval clerk and had hopes of striking it rich. Charles' mom had hopes of becoming a teacher and school director. Dreams of his parents successful livelihoods never happened, in fact they remained poor and struggling to survive.

Things for their family continued to get worse and they had to move to the poor neighborhood, Camden Town, London. Charles' dad had trouble controlling his spending and ended up in jail for living beyond his means and going into debt. When this tragedy happened Charles was 12 years old and he had to quit school and work in a boot-blacking factory. His easy carefree life was over for this 12 year old boy who had to grow up quickly. The rodent infested work place was along the Thames River, where he earned 6 shillings labeling pots filled with fireplace cleaning supplies. Charles, was hurt and felt betrayed by his parents who were suppose to love him and take care of him, but instead he felt betrayed. He never got over this feeling and it became many of the themes in his later writings.

After a few years Charles was able to go back to school when his father receive a family inheritance, allowing his debt to be paid off. He went back to school but his educational dreams was short lived when in 1827 he had to quit school again to help support his 10 family members. The job was a Godsend because it helped him begin his writing career.

Charles continued to do freelance reporting for the London courts. His writing career took off and he began reporting for two London papers. He submitted sketches and articles to various magazines in 1833 under a pen name – Boz. His writings caught the eye of Catherine Hogarth, and a love affair began. They were married for 20 years and had 10 children during that time but they unfortunately divorced in 1858.

Alone, Charles continued writing and sketching and published *The Posthumous Papers of the Pickwick Club*. At this same time Charles was publishing a magazine called *Bentley's Miscellany* and writing his first novel, *Oliver Twist*. This novel mirrored his life, telling about a boy who was an orphan and lived on the street. His difficult life was the theme for many of his novels and writings as he tried to understand being abandoned as a child. Oliver Twist was very successful and Charles continued to try his hand at another successful novels.

From 1838 to 1841 Charles tried to write another novel but was not as successful as *Oliver Twist*. In 1842, Charles and his second wife, Kate, toured the United States speaking and researching American culture. Upon completion of his tour he wrote a sarcastic travelogue, insulting Americans for their culture and materialism.

Charles wrote several more novels, but the one that everyone enjoys is *A Christmas Carol*, where a selfish, curmudgeon miser who has a total change of heart when 3 ghosts visit him in the middle of the night telling him what torment he will endure if he doesn't change his lifestyle. He finally sees the joy life can bring and becomes the most generous, loving man in town.

Charles success from his 76 books earned him $95,000 which made him a millionaire by American standards. Back in London he was recognized by everyone as he walked the streets. Other famous novels penned by Charles are, *A Tale Of Two Cities,* and *Great Expectations.* Teachers assign these famous writings for the life lessons they contain within them.

Charles was in a train accident in 1865 and never fully recuperated, but continued to tour until 1870. That year, at the age of 58, he had a stroke and died at his home in Kent, England. He was buried in Westminster Abby, in the Poet's Corner. At his death he was working on *The Mystery of Edwin Drood,* that was left unfinished.

Activities:

- Search the Internet for A Christmas Carol Trivia and give a prize to the winner.
- Create a reader's theater version of the Christmas Carol assigning parts to willing participants to read.

• Lead a discussion on A Christmas Carol and the lessons we can learn from Scrooge.

• Work the, "A Christmas Carol," Crossword puzzle.

Theme: Macy's Thanksgiving Day Parade

Food:
- Pumpkin pie, pecan pie, pumpkin bread or pumpkin bars.

Crafts:
- Try your hand at some balloon animals. You can use the Internet to find some simple ones to form. Or purchase a balloon animal making kit at a local store or a balloon animal book. Some toy stores have a book of designs that includes balloons. You will need a balloon pump because these balloons are difficult to blow up with your mouth.
- If the budget permits, invite a balloon twister to come and share this art with the group.

History:
As Thanksgiving approaches there is nothing more anticipated then the Macy's Thanksgiving Day Parade. This New York tradition since 1924, has drawn large crowds since the beginning. The first parade reported 3.5 million standing along the parade route not to mention the 50 million TV viewers across the United States. The first parade was held on Christmas day, and it started at Herald Square and traveled to Harlem in Manhattan. The first parade had Macy's employees dressed in fun costumes like cowboys and clowns and also included zoo animals from the New York Central Park Zoo. This 6 mile parade was a fun way to advertise Macy's while celebrating the upcoming holidays season.

This traditions quickly took off and the parade runs every year on Thanksgiving Day marking the beginning of the holiday season. The parade soon displayed large balloon characters that were known by all the spectators. The very first balloon that took flight was Felix the Cat character. After the parade these large balloon characters were let go and whoever retrieved the balloon and brought it back to Macy's would get a prize from Macy's. This process did not seem to be too successful so they discontinued this tradition and deflate the balloons to store for the parade next year.

Another character that floated high above the parade was Bullwinkle the Moose. His flight began in 1961 and can still be seen today. The Great Depression didn't seem to effect the parade-goers, in fact the crowds continued to grow, and grew to more then one million people who attended the parade in New York city during that time. Radio decide to broadcast the parade festivities in 1932. In 1939 as the crowds grew, NBC began to broadcast the parade on TV for all to enjoy viewing the floating balloon characters. Walt Disney didn't want to miss out on the fun, so in 1934 the first Mickey Mouse balloon made his debut at the Thanksgiving Day parade.

The years between 1942 – 1944 was sad for parade-goers because the parade was suspended due to World War II. The organizers donated the rubber from the balloons to the military to make products to use for the war. This parade break was over in 1945 with the end of the war and over 2 million people attended the celebration that year.

This wonderful tradition has been enjoyed by so many over the years and has become a tradition for Americans to view the parade while cooking their Thanksgiving meals. Another fun tradition is watching for your favorite character floating over the parade route each year.

Activities:

- Search the Internet for Fun Facts about the Thanksgiving Day parade to discuss with the group.

- Has anyone in the group attended a Thanksgiving Day parade? What were their experiences and feelings?

- What is it that you are most thankful for?

- Provide paper and pens and lead the group to write a note to someone that they would like to thank. Give some thought to people who provide needed services to us or people who work behind the scenes to make our lives easier, healthier, or more enjoyable but rarely are thanked.

DECEMBER

Theme: Bingo

Food:

- Popcorn, corn dogs or other fair foods and soft drinks.

Craft:

- Get different types of beans and pictures of flowers, roosters, trees or other items that could be decorated with different types of dried beans, peas, and popcorn of different colors. These seeds can be glued to a picture that is mounted on poster board or foam core board that you can find at the dollar store.

History:

Bingo, or should I say Beano, was a game played at country fairs, using cards with numbers on them that participants would cover the numbers with beans. Hence the name, Beano. The numbers would be pulled out of a cigar box. When you got 5 numbers covered in a row, the person would yell "beano" and they would win the prize. The roots of this lotto game came from Italy and was called, *Lo Giuoco del Lotto D'Italia*. This Italian lottery began in 1530 announcing the numbers every Saturday night. Popularity grew for Beano and it spread to France in 1770s, but was called *"Le Lotto."* In France, the game was not for the general public, rather it was a game played by the wealthy population. Beano continued to spread and in the 1800s, its popularity grew to Germany where it was used as a teaching tool for children. When a child played this game it was to help them learn math, spelling, and history.

In 1929, fair-goers in Atlanta, Georgia enjoyed this new fair game "Beano." That same year in New York the game was growing in popularity too. Edwin S. Lowe, a toy salesman, was in the Beano hall enjoying the game when he heard someone misspeak and yelled out "Bingo" instead of "Beano" when they won. Lowes wheel began turning and he decided to change the name and sell it in his toy line. He went a little further, hiring Carl Leffler, a math professor from Columbia University, to make up different numbered playing cards to make the game more challenging for the players. Leffler was said to have created 6,000 different Bingo cards. Lowes new Bingo game took off and spread even more. Rumors said that Leffler went insane - I hope it wasn't from creating the 6,000 different Bingo cards.

Lowe continued to market his Bingo game across America when he met a Catholic priest in Pennsylvania, who thought this game might be a good way to raise money for the church. Many thought this was a wonderful idea, and they began to have Bingo nights at the church. This began in 1930s and by 1934 the church raised much needed funds for the church and its ministries. To date approximately 10,000 games of Bingo are played each week in North America Catholic churches with an estimate earnings for the church of $90 million.

Activities:

- Play Bingo and have prizes for players to win.

Theme: Christmas Around the World

Food:

    • A variety of Christmas cookies, fruitcake, or pastries and cocoa, coffee, Mullen cider, & spice tea.

Craft:

    • Make an Advent wreath using a Styrofoam circle, cuttings of evergreen to stick into the wreath, 1 white candle, 1 pink candle and 3 purple candles for each participant. If you have never seen an Advent wreath look it up on the Internet for examples.

    • Have participants make Christmas cards for family members or friends.

History:

Christmas is celebrated in many different ways around the world and we will look at several countries to learn a little more about the differences.

Africa – An annual Christmas pageant is the tradition in the Congo, performed in the streets of the city. Also groups of carolers walk the streets sharing beautiful music on their way to worship. During the evening worship service, participants bring their offerings to the altar in honor of Jesus' birth. After church, everyone enjoys a Christmas dinner. Families prepare a table on the street in order to invite others to share in their Christmas meal. In South Africa, Christmas is in the summertime so the shared meal is more like a barbeque on the beach or along a river. They may even spend the night camping by the water. The traditional Christmas meal consists of turkey, roast beef, mince pie, or suckling pig, yellow rice with raisins, vegetables and plum pudding.

Australia – Christmas in Australia is in the middle of summer too, which occurs from mid December to early February. Families decorate their houses with lights, wreaths and Christmas trees. Families go caroling around their neighborhoods to spread the Christmas cheer. The state capital has a candlelight service featuring famous Australian singers, the children's entertainers are usually "the Wiggles." Santa visits the children there too, but he uses kangaroos to deliver the presents and wears a cooler outfit instead of the heavy fur outfit. Christmas dinner is usually eaten at lunch time and is either cold food items or a barbecue with seafood, such as prawns or lobster.

Brazil - If you are a child in Brazil you would look for Papai Noel, which their name for Santa Claus. They celebrate in similar ways as we do in the United States. Children leave their socks near the window for Papai Noel to exchange their socks for gifts. Christmas Eve begins the celebration with beautiful fireworks for all to enjoy. A Brazilian Christmas meal includes chicken, turkey, ham, rice, salad, pork, and fresh and dried fruits.

China – In China only 1 percent of the population is Christian, so only those in the cities and shopping malls display Christmas trees. The few individuals who have Christmas trees, decorate them with paper chains, paper flowers, and paper lanterns. Santa is called Sheng dan lao ren which translates to mean Old Christmas Man. The gift the child asks for is gift wrapped and usually given on Christmas Eve. Chinese Christians celebrate Christmas much the same as we do in the United States. People also enjoy caroling, but few understand the songs because they are not believers. The favorite song in China is Jingle Bells.

Denmark - In Denmark, most people begin their Christmas celebration with a 4 PM church service, followed by a family meal that ends with a traditional rice pudding. After dinner, traditionally the family dances around their Christmas tree, followed by opening their presents. These gifts are thought to be brought by Julemanden, Christmas Man, who also travels by a reindeer-pulled sleigh. Julemanden has nissers, his elves, who help him make the toys for children. Some families also exchange gifts on the four Sundays of Advent.

England – Decorating Christmas trees, beautiful music and evergreen branches are all part of the holiday celebration that St Augustine brought to England in 596 AD. Another custom is for people to "mummer," which is when people adorn masks to portray the Christmas plays in the village. Father Christmas wears a green or red robe, while going around leaving presents in children's Christmas stockings or pillowcases, that are hanging on the end of their bed post while they sleep.

France – Nativities are the centerpiece for the Christmas celebrations in France. Joyeux Noel, Happy Christmas is the greeting for the celebration day. Cherry wood Yule logs are carried into the homes at Christmas and doused with red wine, which is thought to make it smell nice. This Yule log and candles are kept burning all night as a custom in case Mary and baby Jesus come past during the night. Pere Noel, the French Santa, delivers gifts to children in the night. The customary Christmas meal consists of roasted turkey or goose with chestnuts, oysters, lobster, venison and cheese, followed by chocolate sponge log shaped cake called buche de Noel. Another traditional practice is having 13 different desserts, made from fruits, nuts, and pastries. This meal is served after Christmas Eve midnight church service.

Germany – In Germany, Advent plays a big role in the celebration. The Advent wreath is made with Fir branches with 24 boxes or bags hanging from it containing presents. Other families make the traditional Advent wreath with a candle for each Sunday of Advent and a white Christ candle. Christmas Trees are another tradition in Germany. Usually the mother of the family secretly decorates the tree, especially if there are young children in the home, as a surprise on Christmas morning. If the children are older, the tree is purchased Christmas Eve and decorated together, followed by reading the Christmas story from the Bible and singing the song Silent Night. Children write letters to Christkind, decorate the envelop with sugar glue to make them sparkle and put them in the windowsill at the beginning of Advent. Gifts are delivered to children on December 24th. Children's school parties and work parties have their gifts tossed in the door, to keep the giver a secret. It is said to be bad luck if you see who delivers the gifts. Another popular tradition is to go door to door singing and collecting money for charity. Four children go around with 3 children dressed as Wise Men and one carries a star on a stick symbolizing the Star of Bethlehem. Before they leave the premises of each home, they write a signature over the door that remains until it wears off. Some traditional foods served are Carp, Goose and Stollen, which is a fruited yeast bread.

Holland – On December 5th, children in Holland are waiting for Sinterklaas to bring them presents. Children leave their shoes by the chimney hoping to get candy left in them. Children hope to hear a knock at the door waiting for

Sinterklaas to leave a sack of gifts for them and their family. Traditional marzipan or pastry are made in the shape of the letter of their family's last name. Christmas day is quieter with a church service and family meal.

India – Celebrations in India are much smaller due to the smaller numbers of Christians there. The largest group is in Bombay, and most are Roman Catholics so midnight mass is very important. After mass the family enjoys a feast of curie dishes. Traditional decorations of poinsettia flowers and candlelight are used in the churches and in family homes. Instead of a pine tree, a banana or mango tree is decorated. Homes in Southern India, put small oil lamps on their roofs signifying that Jesus is the light of the world. Northwest India have groups of people who carol all night, singing the Christmas story in song for all to hear. Santa, Christmas Baba, goes through the streets on a horse drawn carriage deliver gifts to children for their Christmas celebration.

Italy – The tradition of displaying the Nativity at Christmas was brought to Italy in 1223 by St. Francis of Assisi. He visited Bethlehem and became inspired after seeing the stable where Jesus was born. This touched him so much that he brought the importance of the crib to the people in Italy. Every home has a nativity, but baby Jesus is not put in the crib until Christmas Eve. Another tradition is that children would dress in biblical costumes and go around singing and playing shepherds' pipes. After Mass, a meatless meal is served of fish, dairy, a slice of Italian Christmas cake and hot chocolate.

Mexico – The Christmas celebration in Mexico runs from December 12th to January 6th. A traditional practice is for children to dress like Mary and Joseph and go from house to house asking for a room, and the response from within is "no posadas," meaning "no room." Each night after this process a different house hosts the party for the night. On Christmas Eve the final Posada celebration when the baby Jesus is finally put into the nativity and the families goes to church services. After church the family would enjoy a traditional firework display. One of the favorite games at the final Posada is a piñata filled with candy for all to enjoy. The main gifts for children in Mexico are given January 6th at Epiphany, El Dia de los Reyes (the day of The Three Kings). A traditional Kings' cake is enjoyed as part of this celebration party.

Russia - Christmas is not celebrated in Russia much, but those who do, celebrate January 7th at the Catholic Russia Orthodox church. On Christmas Eve they fast and only eat a porridge made from wheat or rice mixed with honey, poppy seeds, dried fruit, walnuts and jellied fruit. Vzvar, a Russian drink, is used to celebrate a birth of a child, so to end their celebration and to honor Jesus' birth, adults have a Vzvar drink. New Years is when Ded Moroz', Father Frost, brings gifts to children after the children circle round the Christmas tree calling for Ded Moroz' to come bring their gifts. There is a folklore that says Babushka, a "witch like," character who bring gifts to the children as she goes through the town sweeping to clean up, preparing for the Wise Men who are looking for Jesus.

Sweden – St Lucy's Day, Christmas in Sweden, is celebrated on December 13th. The brave young Christian girls would bring food to the persecuted Christians, who lived in the Catacombs under the city where they hide. The young girls would wear a evergreen wreath of candles on their head so she could have her hands free to carry the food trays. St. Lucia was one of the young girls killed for her faith. Now the tradition is for young girls to dress in white robes with a red sash and a crown of candles on their head as a reminder of this tradition. The young girls would sing and take ginger snaps to patients in the hospital. A favorite food served for Christmas breakfast is saffron buns with raisins. The big meal is at lunchtime consisting of meatballs, stuffed cabbage rolls, lutfisk (cod with white sauce), jellied pigs feet, oven roasted pork ribs, potatoes and red cabbage. Families make straw goats to guard their Christmas Tree, and also to remind them of Jesus who's bed was a manger filled with straw. Gifts are purchased and delivered by Jultomten, their Santa Claus.

United States – In the United States, our tradition centers around Jesus coming to earth and having been born in a humble stable and laid in a manger, because there was no room for Mary and Joseph in the inn. Mary and Joseph went to Bethlehem because they were taking the census. We celebrate in a beautifully decorated church filled with poinsettias and a Christmas tree filled with Chrismons, which are symbol decorations that represent different names of the attributes of Jesus. We decorate our houses with lights, a Nativity, poinsettias, and a beautifully decorated Christmas tree. Children try to be good all year so that Santa, traveling by a sleigh pulled by reindeer, will deliver gifts to them under their Christmas tree on December 25th. Bad boys and girls get coal in their stocking. Families celebrate with a feast of turkey or ham and all the trimmings. A variety of favorite dessert finish the delicious meal. The best part of the tradition is you spend the season celebrating with family and friends, exchanging gifts and sharing time together making unforgettable memories.

Activities:

- Have different participants read a paragraph about one of the countries listed above. If you have someone from a different country, have them share what they did in their country or look it up and write a small paragraph for them to share.

- Ask each person to share their best Christmas memory with the group.

- Find recipes of Christmas cookies from around the world and prepare a cookie feast to share with local preschoolers or children afterschool. Perhaps you can round out the event by reading the Christmas story and singing carols.

Theme: Christmas Tree History

Food:

- Christmas tree shaped cookies, coffee, tea, cider, and cocoa.

Craft:

Making Christmas Ornaments:

- Ribbon and bead ornaments (see: Pinterest.com) take a 12 inch length piece of ribbon by 1/8 inches wide. Get 10 pearls or beads. Thread a needle with coordinating thread color. Sew through the ribbon about ½ inch from the end of the cut, next thread a pearl on the thread. Then put the needle through the ribbon leaving about 2 inch loop, then thread another pearl on the thread. Continue this process making the loops smaller and smaller as you go along so that it will form Christmas tree ornament.

- Use clear glass balls from a craft store. Get acrylic paint, variety of colors. Have participants drip paint along the inside of the inside of the balls, turning them to disperse the paint inside the ball. More than one color can be used but do not mix too much because it will make a muddy looking ornament. Let them dry and you can add a ribbon bow to the top of the ornament. Or you can embellish the outside with a name or write a greeting with puff paint or gold or silver pens. Or you can free hand designs with puff paints on the outside of a glass ball.

- Make a Snowman ornaments. You use the round or flat glass balls, pour artificial snow flakes inside the ball. Use puff paint to add eyes, nose and mouth of the snowman. You can decorate the the top with a felt hat and ear muffs for added decorations.

History:

Christmas Trees are the centerpiece of the Christmas holiday, that dates back to the 7th century. A monk was teaching in Germany and used a triangle to demonstrate the trinity of God – Father, Son and Holy Spirit. He use a small evergreen tree for his illustration because of its triangular shape, using one corner point for each part of the 3 aspects of God. It was said that he hung the tree upside down from the ceiling to be the focal point of his lecture and he decorated it with symbols of God. Triangles became a symbol for Christianity because of his visual that day. Prior to this event, Europeans would put evergreen branches over their doors and bring evergreen branches inside to decorate their houses for the holiday. The evergreens seemed to lift their spirits during the long winter solstice. Some had superstitions thinking that evergreen branches hanging over their doors would keep away witches, ghosts, evil spirits and illness. The Germans would decorate these trees and branches with apples to signifying the Garden of Eden. Later, nuts, sugar wafers, flowers and tinsel were added to the decorations. Slowly the practice of decorating Christmas tree waned in German.

The Christmas of 1848, the custom of decorating a Christmas tree started up again when Queen Victoria encouraged her husband, Prince Albert, to put up a Christmas tree like he had when he was a child in Germany. They decorated this beautiful tree with sweets, ornaments, candles and topped it with an angel. A picture of their tree ended up in *The Illustrated London News* magazine, and Christmas tree popularity took off again. Britain and America began to display beautifully decorated Christmas trees everywhere. Glass ornaments began being produced in Germany in 1870s which added to the beauty and glow of the trees. Candles were also being used to adorn the trees branches. As concern over the dangers of using candles on Christmas trees, along with the many house fires occurred from this practice, decorating the tree with candles ceased. Twelve years later, Thomas Edison's associate, Edward Johnson, decided to invent the first set of electric Christmas lights. Finally families were able to brighten their Christmas trees again safely with strands of electric lights.

By the 1900s, twenty percent of families had a beautifully displayed Christmas tree in their living rooms. Across the globe over one million Christmas trees were part of the Christmas celebrations. Even President Benjamin Harrison's First lady, began this lovely tradition in 1889 displaying the first Christmas tree in the White House in Washington D.C.

Our Nations Capitol has another traditional that includes 57 beautifully decorated trees called the Pageant of Peace. This lovely display features 56 smaller decorated trees representing all 50 states, five territories, and the District of Columbia, and one large evergreens displayed in the center.

Another large Christmas tree display can be seen in Rockefeller Center in New York city. This magnificent sight is adorned with over 23 thousand Christmas lights and millions of people make a trip to New York to oh and awe over this beautifully decorated tree.

Family traditions consists of many activities during the holidays, but no one is most loved and significant then coming together as a family to decorate the Christmas Tree.

Activities:

- Talk about you favorite Christmas ornament as a child, who gave it to you, what did it look like, and why was it special.

- If possible, decorate a Christmas tree with handmade decorations from participants.

Theme: Boxing Day
December 26

Food:

- Small ham and or turkey sandwiches, small desserts and drinks.

Craft:

- Have the group decorate a jar and write on small pieces of paper nice things they could do for others during the year and put them in the jar. They could sit the jar in their room and pull one out a week or one a month to do something nice for someone.

History:

You won't see people putting on boxing gloves for Boxing Day, but you might see a stack of gifts to distribute to servants and employees to celebrate Boxing Day. This celebration began to honor those who had to work on Christmas day. Families would presented their cooks, housekeepers and servants with a gift as they left the morning of December 26 as they went home to celebrate the holidays with their families. The first group to have celebrated Boxing Day were found during the Middle Ages in Great Britain. Some say that this tradition began in Roman times, when money boxes were displayed for collections at sporting games. This idea was copied by Monks who displayed similar boxes in church for collecting money for the poor. This celebration is also found in the Christmas Carol, *"Good King Wenceslas."* The Duke Of Bohemia saw a poor man gathering wood in the middle of a snowstorm and then he would distribute it to the poor so they would have heat in the snow storm. This story touched the life of the Duke so much that this practice of giving to the poor was incorporated into the celebration. Church-goers during the Christmas holiday would put money into a box for charity and the money was dispersed on December 26th to the poor and needy.

Which story is the truth? It might be all or none, but it is a good way for people to give back to those who serve the public by delivering the mail, serve food, hold doors or others service jobs that take place every day. Churches put the collection box up and worshipers put money into the box for the needy. This holiday is also known as Feast of St. Stephen's Day, named after the Christian martyr who was stoned to death in 415AD for his faith. Stephen was one of the Apostles chosen by Jesus, to help take care of the poor and widows.

Boxing Day traditions of gift giving and collecting money for the poor isn't so popular today in Britain as it use to be. The celebration now consists of a open houses for friends and families to come and visit, eats, watch sports on TV and drink.

This national holiday has been celebrated since 1871 in England, Wales, Ireland and Canada. You will occasionally hear of a Boxing Day celebration in the United States. It is a wonderful way to catch up with friends and neighbors after the hustle bustle of the holiday season has ended. A hundred years ago the historical practice in England for Boxing Day was a fox hunt on December 26th. Parliament banned this well-attended practice of the Boxing Day fox hunt in 2005. Many were troubled by the catching and killing of the fox by the dogs who chased them.

The Irish refer to Boxing Day as St. Stephen's Day and celebrated by holding a mock hunt using fake wren on poles for the hunting dogs to chase. Reports of this practice dates back to 1601, during the Battle of Kinsale. Irish men tried to sneak up on the English to invade their territory, but the call of the wren alerted them of their impending attackers. A killed wren was used initially and paraded through town, but towns people felt this practice was distasteful so it ceased.

Today Boxing Day is celebrated by many by returning Christmas gifts, hunting through the disheveled displays of garments and other items at the department stores, and eating leftovers of turkey dinner and wonderfully decorated desserts. Boxing Day is still celebrated in Britain, Australia, New Zealand, and Canada with food, friends and fun.

Activities:
Sing the Christmas Carol – *"Good King Wenceslas"*

Good King Wenceslas looked out

on the feast of Stephen,

when the snow lay round about,

deep and crisp and even.

Brightly shone the moon that night,

though the frost was cruel,

when a poor man came in sight,

gathering winter fuel.

Hither, page, and stand by me.

If thou know it telling:

yonder peasant, who is he?
Where and what his dwelling?
Sire, he lives a good league hence,
underneath the mountain,
right against the forest fence
by Saint Agnes fountain.
Bring me flesh, and bring me wine.
Bring me pine logs hither.
Thou and I will see him dine
when we bear the thither.
Page and monarch, forth they went,
forth they went together
through the rude wind's wild lament
and the bitter weather.
Sire, the night is darker now,
and the wind blows stronger.
Fails my heart, I know not how.
I can go no longer.
Mark my footsteps my good page,
tread thou in them boldly:
Thou shalt find the winter's rage
freeze thy blood less coldly.
In his master's step he trod,
where the snow lay dented.

Heat was in the very sod
which the saint had printed.
Therefore, Christian men, be sure,
wealth or rank possessing,
ye who now will bless the poor
shall yourselves find blessing

ANSWERS TO WORD SEARCH AND PUZZLES

Solution Pizza Toppings

```
P S E + + + + + + + + + + + + A + +
+ I R G + + + + + P + + + + R N + +
+ + N E A + + + + A + + + + T + C + +
+ + + E P S + + R + + + + I + + H + +
+ + + + A P U M + + + + C + + + O + +
+ + + + + P E A + + + H + + + + V S +
+ + + + + S P P S + O + + + + S I N +
+ + + + I + + L T K + + + + M + E O +
+ + + A + + + + E O + + + O + + S I +
+ + N + + + + H + + H + O I + + + N +
+ S R E P P E P N E E R G N + + + O +
+ + + + + A + + + + H + + O + + + + +
+ + + + R + + + + S + + + R + + + + +
+ + + T + + + + U + + E + E + + + + +
+ + S E O T A M O T S + + P + H + + +
+ + H A M B U R G E R + + P + + A + +
+ + + + + + + + E + + + + E + + + M +
O L I V E S + H + + + + + P + + + + +
+ + + + + + C + + + + + + + + + + + +
```

Alfred Hitchcock Movies

```
+  +  F  F  +  +  +  +  +  +  +  +  +  +  +  +  +  H  N  +  +  +  +
+  +  E  +  R  +  +  T  P  S  Y  C  H  O  +  +  W  +  C  R  O  +  +  +  +
+  +  I  +  +  E  +  +  H  +  +  +  +  +  O  +  U  +  O  R  +  +  +  +
+  +  H  +  +  +  N  +  +  E  +  +  +  D  +  M  +  +  P  T  +  +  +  +
+  +  T  +  +  +  +  Z  +  +  T  +  +  N  +  O  +  +  +  E  H  +  +  +  +
+  +  A  H  +  +  +  +  Y  +  +  H  I  +  O  +  T  +  +  +  B  S  +  +  +
+  T  H  E  T  R  O  U  B  L  E  W  I  T  H  H  A  R  R  Y  Y  U  +  +  +
+  +  C  +  +  I  +  +  +  +  R  +  W  R  E  +  G  +  T  +  N  S  +  +  +
+  +  T  +  +  +  M  +  +  A  +  E  +  L  T  N  +  H  +  +  O  P  +  +  +
E  G  A  T  O  B  A  S  E  +  N  +  A  +  I  Y  E  +  +  +  R  I  +  +  +
+  +  C  +  +  +  +  R  S  K  S  D  +  R  +  B  N  +  +  +  T  C  +  +  +
+  +  O  +  +  +  +  +  O  R  Y  P  E  +  I  +  +  I  +  +  H  I  +  +  +
O  +  T  +  +  +  H  +  V  M  H  E  R  +  +  +  +  N  +  W  O  +  +  +
G  +  +  +  +  W  +  A  +  T  D  D  L  +  +  +  +  +  E  E  N  +  +  +
I  +  +  +  +  N  +  N  +  +  +  S  N  +  L  +  +  +  +  +  S  +  +  +
T  +  +  F  A  M  I  L  Y  P  L  O  T  A  +  B  +  +  +  +  T  T  +  +
R  +  +  M  +  S  +  +  +  +  +  +  +  R  +  O  +  +  +  +  +  E  +  +
E  +  E  +  H  +  +  +  +  +  +  +  +  +  M  A  U  +  +  +  +  +  P  +
V  H  +  E  +  +  +  +  +  +  +  +  +  +  +  C  N  +  +  +  +  +  S
T  +  S  T  B  U  O  D  A  F  O  W  O  D  A  H  S  +  C  D  +  +  +  +  +
+  +  +  +  +  +  +  +  +  +  +  +  +  +  +  +  +  +  E  +  +  +  +
+  +  +  +  +  +  +  +  +  +  +  +  +  +  +  +  +  +  +  B  +  +  +
+  +  +  +  +  +  +  +  +  +  +  +  +  +  +  +  +  +  +  +  E  +  +  +
+  +  +  +  +  +  +  +  +  +  +  +  +  +  +  +  +  +  +  +  +  R  +  +
```

Winnie the Pooh

```
C + S + + + + T + + + + + + + + S + + +
+ H + P + + I + + + + + + R + + R + + +
+ + R + M G + + + + + + + A + + A + + +
W + + I G U + + S + + + + B + + L + + +
I + + E S + L E + + + + + B + + U + + +
N + R + + T L A E + + + + I + + G + + +
N + + + + Z O + F E + + + T + + A + + +
I + + + O + + P + F Y + + + + + J + + +
E + + O + + + + H + E O A G N A K + + +
T + W + + + + + + E T H R + + + + + + +
H + + E + + + + + H R + + E + + + + + +
E + E + + + + + E + + R + + + + + + + +
P B + + + + + B + + + + O + + + + + + +
O + + + + + A + + + L + + B + + + + + +
O + + + + C + + + + W + + + I + + + + +
H + + + K + T R E B O R E L C N U + + +
+ + + S + + + + + + + O + + + + S + + +
+ + O + + + + + + + + + R + + + + + + +
+ N + + + + + + + + + + + + + + + + + +
S + + + + + P I G L E T + + + + + + + +
```

227

Sesame Street Characters

```
T + + + + + + M + + + + + + C
R + + + Y + + U + + + + + T O
E + + + + L + P + + + + N + O
B + + + + + L P + + + U + + K
O S C A R T H E G R O U C H I
+ + + + G + + T T C + + + Y E
+ + + + + R + + E + + + + E M
+ + + + + + O H + + + R + L O
+ + + + + + T V + + O + + I N
+ B I G B I R D E S + + + M S
+ + + + + + + + I R O + + S T
G O R F E H T T I M R E K Y E
E I N R E + A + L + Z O E U R
+ + + + + + + E + + + + + G +
+ + + + + + + + + + + + + +
```

Famous Couples
(fill in the blanks)

1. Romeo _____ Juliet
2. Lucy Ball _____ Desi Arnaz
3. Fred Flinstone _____ Wilma Flitstone
4. Ethel Mertz _____ Fred Mertz
5. Barney Rubble _____ Betty Rubble
6. Cleopatra _____ Mark Antony
7. George Burns _____ Alicie Allen
8. Richard Burton _____ Elizabeth Taylor
9. Scarlett O'Hara _____ Rhett Butler
10. Adam _____ Eve
11. Odyssesus _____ Penelope
12. Brad Pitt _____ Angelina Jolie
13. Bonnie Parker _____ Clyde Barrow
14. Demi Moore _____ Ashton Kutcher
15. Elvis Presley _____ Pricilla Presley
16. Franklin Roosevelt _____ Eleanor Roosevelt
17. George W. Bush _____ Laura Bush
18. George Washington _____ Martha Washington
19. Goldie Hawn _____ Kurt Russell
20. Ike Eisenhower _____ Mamie Eisenhower
21. Jennifer Garner _____ Ben Affleck
22. Jennifer Lopez _____ Marc Anthony
23. John F. Kennedy _____ Jackie Kennedy
24. John Lennon _____ Yoko Lennon
25. John Travolta _____ Kelly Preston
26. Roy Rogers _____ Dale Evans
27. Ronald Reagan _____ Nancy Reagan
28. Sonny _____ Cher
29. Barbie _____ Ken
30. Beauty _____ Beast

Aurora Memorial Library
115 E. Pioneer Trail
Aurora, OH 44202

08012018

9 781621 376941